T5-AXH-643

Brenda & Milton

June 2018

Happy trails today and always!

Shelley Lance-Fulk & Jacklyn Amtower

CAN I CARRY YOUR LUGGAGE?

*Tales Behind the Wildlife Photos Taken
by Two Sisters Traveling the World*

SHELLEY LANCE-FULK
& JACKLYN AMTOWER

COMPASS ROSE IMAGES
BEAVER COVE, MAINE

CAN I CARRY YOUR LUGGAGE?
Tales Behind Wildlife Photos Taken by Two Sisters Traveling the World
©2017 Shelley Lance-Fulk and Jacklyn Amtower

ISBN 13: 978-1-63381-107-2

All rights reserved. No part of this publication may be reproduced (except for reviews), stored in a retrieval system, or transmitted in any form by any means, electronic, mechanical, photocopying, recording or other, without the written prior permission of the publisher and/or author.

All Photographs ©2017 Compass Rose Images

designed and produced by
Maine Authors Publishing
12 High Street, Thomaston, Maine 04861
www.maineauthorspublishing.com

Printed in the United States of America

This wildlife photography journal is dedicated to those with whom we have traveled and others who we have yet to meet.

THERE IS NO NEED TO PACK YOUR BAGS, UPDATE YOUR PASSPORT OR STAND in line for airport screenings. Grab your favorite beverage, sit in your favorite chair and join us for a wildlife adventure around the world. We hope our tales and recollections, along with some of our favorite photographs, will encourage you to explore the world of animals in the future. We hope to meet you as our journey continues....

CONTENTS

CAN I CARRY YOUR LUGGAGE?

INTRODUCTION

OUR STORY BEGINS NOT WHERE YOU MIGHT IMAGINE. ALTHOUGH WE began our wildlife photographic safaris in earnest a decade ago, our journeys combining our love of animals and photography started when we were young girls growing up in Southern California (yes, an unlikely spot for our beginning).

We began traveling internationally in our teens, in the mid-1960s, when our father, having been raised in an orphanage in New York, couldn't get a passport without a birth certificate. Our parents had to make a decision either to cancel a planned trip to Europe or to permit their two teenage girls (Jacklyn, age 19 and Shelley, age 15) to go in their stead. Against their better judgment, and with much trepidation and continual urging by us, they chose the latter. Our first trip set the stage for our later obsession with travel. With our Kodak Instamatic camera, dozens of rolls of film, and considerable excitement, we flew to Europe with a tour group to experience life abroad. As we were by far the youngest travelers, it didn't take us long to decide to leave the group and set out on our own, never expecting the tour leader to report our absence to our parents back in California.

In those days before cell phones and internet, the only way to communicate was via telephone, mail, or telegram. We chose to send a telegram informing our parents of our plans and assuring them we were safe. Although we knew we would be in big trouble upon our return (yes we were!), we ventured forth for four weeks of adventure taking trains, buses, ferries, and taxis. We knew we had to rejoin our group for the return flight home, so right on time, we re-

turned to Paris. With hundreds of photos of local—mostly farm—animals, including sheep, horses, donkeys, birds, and cows, we fell in love with animal photography. We did return home safely with numerous stories and a few tales to tell to our angry and worried parents who anxiously demanded, "What were you thinking?"

Developing film in those days was hit or miss and quite costly. We never had a darkroom, so not only would we have to purchase the film, we would then have to take our film to a photo shop for developing. The rolls of film did not hold many images, perhaps 12 or 20 shots, so carrying many rolls on a trip was a necessity. Often you would return from your travels and develop the film, only to find that many of the shots were out of focus, poorly framed, or just plain bad. You couldn't go back and take the photos again. You might have great memories of the trip, but with nothing to share.

It took us longer than most to convert from film to digital photography, but once we began shooting digitally, we never looked back. The definition, color, and clarity coupled with our ability to take unlimited shots and delete most of them, made travel photography easier and the outcome more assured. All we need in addition to the camera are tiny memory cards that hold a thousand or more photos. Now, unfortunately, the number and weight of the assortment of lenses we carry cause other types of issues.

Jacklyn met her husband, Jon, on a polar bear expedition in Svalbard, a remote island off the northern coast of Norway. Jon is a marine engineer—first as a submariner in the US Navy and then as a chief engineer with NOAA—who did oceanographic research all over the world. He's not a photographer but travels with us whenever a location interests him. Jon suggested our company's name, Compass Rose Images, which is a reflection of our worldwide travels. The compass rose is a nautical term, and its image, when viewed as a circle on a chart, points in all directions—our desired travel locations.

Shelley's husband, Eric, never cared to leave the States and preferred exploring our country by car whenever possible. Shelley lived in the Phoenix area, and when Eric passed away, she relocated to Beaver Cove, Maine, to live with Jacklyn and Jon. With all three of us sharing an obsession with travel, it seemed only natural that we would eventually travel, photograph our favorite animals, and share with others our commitment to respect and protect our world's precious gifts through our photography. We love what we are privileged to do. We travel four to six months a year and have no plans to change our lives.

Both of us shoot with Canon DSLR cameras with a variety of lenses ranging from 18mm to 1000mm. We like using a zoom lens as much as possible for greater flexibility. Although we have different camera bodies, we are able to interchange our lenses, depending upon our situation or need. When we travel, we take along a variety of lenses, numerous memory cards, and two iPads onto which we download our photos each night for review, so if necessary (and possible), we may repeat a shot the next day.

Historically, travel was undertaken for the purpose of trade or other utilitarian reasons. The first recorded experiences of those who traveled for exploration was in the second century. Travel journals and artist's drawings documented new sights and destinations and piqued an interest in seeing the world. Those who must travel for business often view it as an unpleasant necessity, whereas those of us who travel for fun see the long plane or sea trips as an opportunity for new adventures and experiences. We consider each trip a privilege and an opportunity to observe new environments, cultures, and wildlife, and to use our good fortune in a meaningful way. We love to share our observations and memories, especially with those who are unable to travel but can live vicariously through our stories and images. Our photographs hopefully add to the understanding of a greater world and an appreciation and respect for the animals that enrich our lives.

Depending on the type of trip, we plan our journeys accordingly. When traveling to the Polar Regions such as Antarctica or the Arctic, it is necessary for us to use a medium-sized expedition ship or icebreaker, whereas in the Galápagos, for example, we travel on very small vessels, often carrying fewer than 20 passengers. In Africa, we prefer to go to a region and book a guide and tracker with a vehicle for the greatest flexibility. First-time visitors to Africa generally have time limits and want to see as many animals as possible. Using our own guides, we are able to spend as much time with a particular animal as we wish. This was the case as we sat in our vehicle for three hours awaiting the birth of a rhino calf.

We have traveled to approximately 75 countries on all seven continents. This number does not include individual islands or territories of the above-named countries such as the many Galápagos Islands (Ecuador), the Seychelles (off eastern Africa), the Isle of Skye (Scotland), or islands like Komodo (Indonesia), Jeju (South Korea), or Moorea (French Polynesia). Unfortunately, the list of places we wish to visit never gets any shorter. And the more we talk with our fellow travelers, the more we discover other places to add to our "must-see" list. As we attend weekly art shows to display our work, we always seem to learn of new animals whose images we would like to capture.

People frequently ask us, "What is your favorite place?" Our response is usually some variation on "wherever we are at the time," but both Antarctica and South and East Africa are certainly at the top of our list. The remoteness and splendor of the icebergs and the overwhelming number of penguins, whales, seals, and seabirds make a dangerous sea trip to the south a thrill unlike any other. Africa, with its vast plains, wonderful people, and tremendous number of large and small wildlife creatures, is an adventure in sensory overload. We tend to go to different countries in Africa each year, spending a couple of months at a time. For elephant photos we like to shoot in Botswana, but for leopards we choose Zambia. We prefer shooting our African flamingos in Namibia or Tanzania and our King penguins in the Falkland Islands or the Antarctic. For birds, we choose the South Pacific, the Amazon, or South America.

Another popular question is how close we can get to the animals. It varies. Birds in flight are always a challenge and are usually photographed from a distance using a long lens. Keeping a large, heavy lens stationary is difficult. You learn fairly quickly that you don't try to chase a bird across the sky with your lens but rather anticipate its flight path, pre-focus on where the bird might pass, adjust the speed and focus settings, and wait. Sometimes you get lucky!

Even in a vehicle in Africa, the motor is usually kept running in anticipation of a quick escape. Should an animal charge, we can move away quickly. The vibration of the vehicle causes the camera to move, so adjustments must be made with a faster shutter speed to preclude blurring or out-of-focus shots. During the day it is possible to approach even predatory mammals within a few feet, enabling the use of a shorter (and much lighter) lens. Close-up photos are the best, as you can capture the souls of the animals through their eyes and faces. When you walk among the penguins, seals, and seabirds of Antarctica or the Galápagos, the wildlife is right at your feet, so you can use a short lens. Giraffes, on the other hand, are a real challenge to photograph. If you are close to a towering giraffe, you must choose either to concentrate on a head shot with a mid-range lens or try to capture the entire animal with a short lens, but the latter is nearly impossible if you are really close. Photographing polar bears offers an entirely different challenge. When walking along the tundra in their territories, always protected by guides with rifles to shoot in the air should a bear approach, the sighting of a polar bear provides us with a single opportunity. You need to take the photo from a distance with a long lens and then immediately hop back into Zodiacs to be shuttled back to the expedition ship for safety. Fortunately, when they are on the ice, the bears often come close to our vessels, perhaps smelling the food being prepared for our meals. Our ships can usually approach the bears rather closely.

We are also frequently asked if we have had any close calls with the animals, especially in Africa. The only real problems have involved encounters with people in some of the larger cities, and during actual travel. Traveling by plane, ship, train, and motor vehicle in remote areas of the world always holds the potential for accidents or injuries. We have had rough sea crossings in and around the Southern (Antarctic) Ocean and the Bering Sea, a near midair collision, and erratic drivers in taxis where we hung on for our lives. Our precarious situations in the wild are less frequent, though memorable, and include being bitten by a scorpion in a remote area of Africa, being surrounded by a large group of elephants protecting their young, and suffering an attack in an enclosed space by hundreds of tsetse flies.

We attend juried and non-juried art shows each weekend during our season, which usually runs from the end of April through November. It is wonderful knowing that our pictures and stories reach others throughout the world. Our website now has hundreds of photos, so it is hard to choose which animal images to enlarge, use for coasters or trivets, or highlight at our weekly shows. If the most popular photos are wolves one week, we bring additional wolves the following week, only to find that the favored animal is a giraffe. We have had the same problem selecting which photos to include within this book. Often a child will come to our display looking for a photo of a rabbit, a golden retriever, or a hamster. We may have photos of sloths, hartebeest, lemurs, or Gentoo penguins, but not hamsters. Every week is an adventure trying to meet the interests of our show patrons.

All our pictures have stories associated with them. When a particular image piques the interest of one of our patrons, we share the story behind the picture so that when the individual returns home or offers the photo product as a gift, the story makes the photo more meaningful. We have many stories, some humorous and interesting and a few that are frightening, that we will share within this book.

The book's title reflects the most often repeated question that arises at our weekly art shows: "Can I carry your luggage?" First we are asked whether we took all the photos on display, and when we say yes, the offer to carry our luggage, cameras, or equipment follows. Other questions arise as to where we have been, when we travel, how we get there, and whether we are afraid to go. Those who choose not to travel or who are unable to visit faraway locales nevertheless love to hear the stories behind the images. We have had so many people wanting to go with us and assist us by carrying our luggage that we thought this would be an appropriate title.

We welcome input from both our patrons and those who read this retelling of our stories as to which animals we should photograph in the future. We try to schedule our adventures based on input we receive. As travel has become more difficult in some regions of the world due to safety or other travel restrictions, we move those locations to the back burner in hopes that situations may change and enable us to visit in the future. We would love to photograph the okapi in the Democratic Republic of the Congo and the great apes in Rwanda, but State Department warnings in the past have precluded this. Last year we were scheduled to visit Senegal, Gambia, and Ghana in western Africa, but the Ebola outbreak necessitated a change in plans. We were likewise scheduled to visit Phuket a few days after the tsunami hit, and the east coast of Japan just after the Fukushima nuclear disaster. Both trips had to be rescheduled. We have since returned to Thailand and Japan, and our plans in 2017 once again include Japan to photograph snow monkeys and cranes.

We will share some of our most memorable stories and photographs, which hopefully illustrate our joy in experiencing the best our world has to offer. Should any of our readers have questions or suggestions about our past or future travel, we encourage your comments and input, guidance and insight. Please visit our website and like us on Facebook, as new pictures are added whenever we travel. Thank you for letting us share our good fortune and wonderful experiences with you.

OUR FAVORITE CONTINENTS AND THE PLACE WE CALL HOME

THE FOCUS OF OUR PHOTOGRAPHY HAS BEEN WILDLIFE, ALTHOUGH we shoot images of people, flowers, and landscapes for our own enjoyment, so we have included a few other photos to complement our travel journal. Animals in the wild have proven to be the most interesting to viewers on our website and those attending our art fairs. Wildlife photos from Africa, Australia, and Antarctica seem to be the most popular. On the following pages, we will share our experiences and photos from these and other areas of the world. We hope you enjoy our adventure stories and experiences so that you will plan a trip of your own.

AFRICA

WE FIND THE LARGEST NUMBER AND VARIETY OF WILDLIFE IN THIS southern continent. It is the second largest and the most populous in the world, and its biodiversity is tremendous. Africa boasts a large population of cats, including lions, cheetahs, servals, and leopards. In addition, it has herbivores such as antelope, elephants, and camels, as well as reptiles, primates, other jungle animals, and aquatic life—and most are found nowhere else on this planet. The tourist usually comes to this continent to observe the big five: the Cape (African) buffalo, elephant, rhino, lion, and leopard. The term *big five* does not refer to the size of the animal but rather to the fact that these used to be the most favored hunting trophies. Africa is also home to the "little five" that include the buffalo weaver, elephant shrew, rhinoceros beetle, ant lion, and leopard tortoise.

Of all the big cats, the cheetah is one of our favorites. It is the world's fastest animal, and can run up to seventy miles an hour when chasing its prey. Cheetahs are a bit smaller than lions and taller than leopards, and are easily recognized by their spotted coats and the black, tear-drop marking that streaks their faces from the inner corner of the eye to the corner of the mouth. They hunt by vision rather than by scent during the day in dry forests, bushy areas, and flat plains. Once their preferred prey (gazelle or impala) is caught, the cheetah begins eating immediately from the rear of the animal. As they do not protect their prey well from other animals such as hyenas, cheetahs try to eat the most nutritious part as fast as they can, before other carnivores drive them away.

We were very fortunate to have been able to get close to two young cheetahs in a rescue facility in South Africa. These two six-month-old brothers had lost their mother to predation and were being cared for until they could be released back into the wild. We entered a large enclosure where the cubs immediately approached us, not unlike domestic housecats. We spent close to thirty minutes with them, kicking around soccer balls and other objects to encourage their play. We found their coats to be smooth and fairly soft, though while petting these cats, we were very mindful of their sharp teeth. It was a wonderful experience to be able to get so close to these magnificent animals.

In school, we were always taught that lions do not climb trees. Unlike leopards, they lack retractable claws, which would seem to make climbing trees impossible. This was not the case in the Tanzanian Serengeti. On one of our first trips to East Africa, we were driving to try to identify the six large animals within the branches of a tree, and were thrilled to see lions sitting calmly amid the branches. We had heard stories about tree-climbing lions in Africa and were excited to find them on this first trip and on several occasions thereafter.

In the Serengeti, lions are able to "climb" the large, gnarled-branched sausage tree, whose low profile enables them to jump from lower to higher branches without difficulty. The sausage tree (Kigelia) has pendulum-like fruits hanging from its branches. These fruits are fibrous and contain pulp and seeds which are eaten by many animals, including birds. Natives in the area also use the fruit for skin products, as vessels for carrying liquids, and to make an alcoholic beverage. The tree's trunk is used for boats and other products. As the fruit is poisonous to humans, it must be dried, roasted and then allowed to ferment before being consumed.

Lions in this area climb these trees for obvious reasons. Lions may rest in a tree to avoid other predators, few of which climb trees. They then have a distinct advantage of sight from above. Lions have excellent senses of smell and vision, so they can spot distant prey sooner. The lioness resting on the branch was one of six other cats in her

pride above her in this tree. This young cat, seeing the others above, began leaping up the tree branches with ease. Suddenly, as if instantly fatigued, she plopped down and rested in this position, just in time for our shot of the day!

Lions live and work within a pride's social hierarchy, consisting of a dominant male and his harem of females and cubs. A single lion is most apt to hunt during the day, but at night the pride works cooperatively to stalk, chase, and capture the prey by circling the targeted animal. This photo was taken of a large male lion that approached our vehicle early one morning during our sunrise drive. We were a bit anxious as he crept closer to us. When he reached the side of the vehicle, he sat down calmly. We were four feet from this large predator, but as he seemed not to show any interest in us, we sat equally quietly and took his photograph. He was very interested, however, in the vultures that were circling above. Several yards to the right we noticed movement and saw the rest of his pride eating their prey. "Our" lion had apparently had his fill and was resting, quite comfortably, just a few feet from us.

The leopard is Shelley's favorite animal. From our very first trip, the leopard has always remained at the top of our list to photograph. Unlike the cheetah, the leopard has a large head, short legs, and markings shaped like rosettes that are clear in the center. The leopard is primarily nocturnal, and with its retractable claws, is able to drag its prey up a tree, which is where we usually spot it. The leopard is very agile and powerful but considerably slower than a cheetah. As these cats are territorial, even though our guides are able to take us to areas where they might be spotted, sightings are few. It is always a bonus to come upon a leopard, either on land or hanging in a tree. We have been fortunate to encounter many leopards in Kenya, Tanzania, and especially in Zambia.

While driving in search of animals to photograph in Tanzania, we came upon two young male leopards walking just in front of our vehicle. We took initial photos and then watched them as they circled about the area, seemingly without direction. Our guide said that these two were old enough to leave their mother's protection and were probably recently sent out, as adults, to hunt alone. Eventually these two young males will find their own territories and claim a female to continue their life's cycle.

The following day we were unbelievably fortunate and excited to come upon a mating pair of leopards in a tree, several yards from where we were passing. We had all we could do to keep quiet. It was more likely that a solitary animal would be spotted. The leopard typically hunts at night, and it is quite rare to find a breeding pair in the daytime. We spent a great deal of time watching them walk along the branches, appearing to hug each other and to exhibit the type of mating behavior seen in humans. We cherish this photo of the mating pair and hope in the future we can again witness such a beautiful encounter. Because of Shelley's overwhelming mission to view and photograph these animals, she is now known by our guides as "Mama Chui," the Swahili term for Mother Leopard!

The African elephant is the largest land mammal in the world and is easily differentiated from the Asian species by its size, large ears, and absence of hair. Its trunk, which acts as a fifth limb, amplifies sound and assists with feeding and touch. Elephants replace their teeth four to six times over their lifetime, but when they reach 40 to 60 years of age, they lose the last of their molars and eventually die of starvation. Both males and females have tusks that are used for stripping the bark off trees. Their family group is matriarchal and is comprised of several females and calves, led by the eldest female. Elephants are intelligent and exhibit behaviors such as learning, sadness, humor, the use of objects, and cooperation. They also have an excellent memory.

One guide explained how elephants remember their dead. When a herd member dies, others attempt to arouse the motionless animal. In some instances, they will use their tusks to dig a shallow grave and toss leaves and small branches on the body. The herd will remain with the deceased throughout the night, and whenever they return to the same area over the years, they will momentarily pause to pay their respects.

One of our most memorable experiences occurred as we were being taken down the Kafue River in Zambia in a small wooden canoe. Ahead of us, we saw what appeared to be the end of an elephant's trunk and a gray lump, swimming below the surface of the water. Just before we approached, the animal reached the other end of the waterway and began to rise. The large animal swimming was indeed an elephant, a bit too close to us for comfort. We snapped a few shots and backed away as it turned toward us in a posturing manner. The photo shows the elephant just as it began to surface. It was an awesome sight.

The giraffe is always a favorite and usually will bring a smile to the faces of both young and old. With its long neck and legs, its distinctive coat pattern and peculiar gait, the giraffe is easily recognizable, though its pattern varies among the four species. Its gait is unique in that, rather than alternating steps with each of its four feet, it moves its legs first on one side and then the other. Because of its long neck, its blood pressure

is a concern. The giraffe's head must not be lowered for long periods of time or the blood pressure drops and the animal may lose consciousness. They are most often seen while standing or semi-kneeling to drink, but do, on occasion, rest on the ground. Giraffes are browsers and extend their large purple tongues to pull twigs, leaves, bark, and fruit from the acacia tree.

Giraffes are becoming endangered in the wild. Although we can view giraffes frequently when traveling in the southern regions of Africa, we were able to visit a giraffe center in Nairobi where the Rothschild giraffe, a subspecies of the northern giraffe, is protected, and where efforts are being made to reintroduce these unusual and rare giraffes back into the wild. Only 1500 of these unique animals remain in the world. They are a bit larger that the Maasai or reticulated giraffe, are paler in color, and have no markings below the knee, as if they were wearing white knee socks. They are prone to hybridization, so reestablishing the population of the Rothschild has been difficult. They may be seen in the wild in Lake Nakuru National Park in Kenya and in the northern part of Uganda.

This picture is of Betty, one of the prized Rothschild giraffes at the center. She was quite friendly, having had many interactions with tourists, and was more than willing to take food from our hands. Her rough, dark purplish tongue, approximately twenty inches in length, constantly reached for our treats. What a pleasure it was to be able to look into Betty's dark inquisitive eyes at close range.

A frequently-asked question is, "Are zebras white with black stripes or black with white stripes?" Zebras have been shown embryologically to have black backgrounds with white stripes, but each animal has its own pattern. They live in large herds or harems and often are seen with wildebeest and small antelopes such as gazelles or impalas. Generally one male and up to six females live together in the harem. The group is very protective of their young and circles the foals when a predator is in the area. Zebras sleep standing up and rely heavily on alarms from other animals during this period. It is thought that the stripes serve several important survival purposes, including confusing a predator by making a single zebra hard to identify within the herd. The stripes may also offer a clue to identification within the herd, and some studies indicate that the stripes thermoregulate the animal with air responding differently to each color. Zebras have excellent hearing and eyesight.

The Cape buffalo is a very menacing and dangerous animal with a prominent horn that is fused with the skull, forming a single structure known as a boss. As the horn begins to grow with the animal, it becomes more curved. It is not unusual to

see younger calves with straight horns. Although they look somewhat like domestic cattle, they are not related, cannot be domesticated, and have few predators, other than lions, that challenge them. They are large mammals that can reach up to 2,000 pounds. A herd is made up primarily of related females and their calves, with the males and older animals surrounding them. Buffaloes take care of each other by responding to a distress call through "mobbing" behavior to fight off predators, and will act in concert should a young buffalo need rescuing.

One of the most dangerous and unpredictable animals in Africa is the hippopotamus. Although an herbivore, it is responsible for thousands of human deaths each year. It is often referred to as the "river horse." It is semi-aquatic and seen in and around rivers and lakes. Hippos can reach close to 3,300 pounds but are capable

of running 20 miles per hour on land. During the day, they can be seen semi-submerged with just their massive heads above water, remaining cool and protecting their sensitive skin. They leave the water in the evening to graze on grasses. They are not social animals and though they sometimes huddle together in the water, the only bonds are between mothers and daughters. The males are territorial in the water with a single bull controlling an area with numerous females.

A massive land beast sought after by photographers is the rhinoceros, easily recognizable by its large, single horn. As herbivores, they eat a diet of fruits, twigs, grasses and leaves and avoid all meat, so it is not necessary for them to hunt. There are several types of rhinos in the world, but only the black rhino (smaller than the white and with a pointed mouth) and the white rhino (square mouth and muscular hump) live in Africa. The black rhino is endangered. Rhinos are a real target for poaching. Their horns are perceived to be an aphrodisiac in parts of Asia and an antidote to poison in Yemen and Oman. Other cultures believe the horn may cure cancer. None of these presumptions are true, so the elimination of the exploitation of this animal has been a major initiative of many governments and rescue projects around the world.

Botswana is a country known for its elephants. While on our way to a watering hole where large numbers of elephants usually are found, we came upon a pack of African wild or painted dogs. These dogs, which are found in many areas of Sub-Saharan Africa, are mangy-looking with stiff, brush-like, brown and black fur. They are lean with long legs, large ears, and a black muzzle. They are highly social animals and live in groups of up to two dozen, mostly in dry, flat environments. The African wild dog is intelligent and cooperative in their hunting and eating behavior.

A pack of African wild dogs we came upon was amazing to watch. Four of the dogs were consuming a recently killed animal. We noticed other dogs standing watch from a distance and one lone dog far from the meal. We were astounded to observe one of the dogs that had been eating, pick up a muscled bone and trot the large bone to the far sentry so he too could share in the meal! This cooperative behavior was repeated with the other dogs protecting the meal.

Several days later, in Zimbabwe, we were able to visit an African wild dog rescue facility. It is not uncommon for these interesting animals to become ensnared in wire traps set primarily by poachers hoping to trap larger animals. The dogs in this facility are rehabilitated and returned to the wild. One of our most prized possessions is a sculpture of a wild dog made from a wire snare removed from one of the animals. This reminder of our responsibility to protect wildlife, whenever and wherever possible, hangs in a prominent place in our home.

Although a large variety of monkeys and apes are found throughout Africa, the vervet monkey is one of our favorites. These white primates with black faces have been studied as a model for understanding both human behavior and genetics. They live in large groups and are very vocal with one another and when predators are nearby. Their society is hierarchal, but males and females form their own social structure and dominance. They are used to humans and are frequently found around tent camps, often harassing and stealing objects from tourists. The photo of a vervet monkeys illustrate common behavior between humans and these primates in their resting and observing habits.

Another primate of note is the lemur, found on the African island of Madagascar. Interestingly enough, these animals did not arise from monkeys or apes but evolved independently due to the isolation of the island. Two thousand years ago, lemurs were the size of apes. They have wet noses and an acute sense of smell which is used to complement their poorer sense of vision. Plants, fruits, and insects make up their diet. Lemurs live in small social groups, with behaviors varying by whether the lemur is nocturnal or diurnal. Their long, powerful back legs enable them to jump great distances and land upright, clinging to the next tree. The photo of Shelley with the lemurs illustrates one of our most comical encounters. Shelley was sitting and resting on a rock in an area where

lemurs were present. When a female with a pup clinging to her belly jumped onto Shelley's shoulder, it was as if the female wanted to show off her baby. Within the span of a minute, other lemurs were leaping on Shelley. One lemur in particular began grooming her and looked as if it was pulling ticks from her hair!

There are few photos that elicit the comment, "You must be kidding" more than the ones of the goats in a tree in Morocco. While driving on the road to Marrakesh, we spotted large, unidentifiable objects in distant trees. As we got closer, the objects revealed themselves to be goats. The argan trees of Morocco are often littered with hungry goats, which climb or perch on the trees in search for nuts. This tree's fruit crop (the nut) is a favorite of the local goats who swarm the branches. The fruits' seeds are then used to create argan oil which is used in cooking and beauty products. When the goats digest and excrete the fruit after eating, the seeds are removed, and first dried in the open air. The fleshy pulp is then extracted and the kernels removed. The kernels are then roasted, ground, and then pressed by hand by a cooperative of Berber women, to recover the essential oil used to make shampoo and cosmetics.

AUSTRALIA/NEW ZEALAND

W E HAVE VISITED AUSTRALIA AND NEW ZEALAND ON MULTIPLE occasions, but the desire to return again never fades. Australia is the sixth largest country in the world, and its biodiversity is tremendous. With the world's largest coral reef, the outback's desert-like plains, rain forests, mountains, and islands such as Tasmania, Australia is a photographer's dream. There are few places that offer more diverse wildlife: kangaroos, wallabies, wombat, koala, emu, kookaburra, crocodiles, dingo, and a variety of sea life.

As much as we enjoy visiting Australia, living there would elicit fear of the smaller creatures including a large numbers of poisonous snakes and spiders (530 species), the wildlife we try to avoid! On one of our trips, we spoke with a couple from Melbourne who shared two stories of animals we both fear. We learned of a large wolf spider (its body was over an inch in diameter) that was found in one of the woman's kitchen cabinets. Seeing its eight eyes set in three rows, she immediately closed the cabinet door and taped it shut. Years later she still has not reopened that door! Another story was one of a carpet python that appeared in a neighbor's yard and consumed

the neighbor's small dog. Sometimes the smallest creatures are the ones that cause the greatest concern!

The koala, an adorable marsupial, is easily identified by its snout, tailless body, and round fluffy ears. Koalas are usually found in woodlands of eucalyptus trees. Due to the limited nutritional value of the their diet of eucalyptus leaves, koalas sleep up to twenty hours per day; therefore, we often see koalas clinging to trees when we are walking or driving through forested areas. The koala's gestation period is between 33 and 35 days, and the young are born while still in the embryonic stage. The baby, known as a joey, continues to develop over a period of six months until it begins to poke its head from its mother's pouch. At nine months, it leaves the protection of the mother's pouch, but it is not fully weaned until a year old.

The kangaroo is another entertaining animal to observe and photograph. Also a marsupial, it is the largest of the species endemic to Australia. The large, powerful back legs and large feet are adapted for leaping, while the long, muscular tail is used for balance. Like cattle, the kangaroo has chambered stomachs and regurgitates the vegetation it has eaten, chews it as cud, and then swallows it for digestion. The kangaroo group or mob is made up of a dozen or more animals. As they are so prolific throughout Australia, care must be taken on roads. Kangaroos may reach speeds of 30 miles per hour and are able to jump great distances, so they are sometimes caught mid-jump when vehicles are passing.

In New Zealand, no matter where we traveled, we saw tremendous numbers and varieties of sheep grazing on farms. These sheep, used for wool products and meat, form a significant industry in the New Zealand economy. Other animals such as sea and land birds (some flightless such as the kiwi), seals, penguins, and reptiles add to the abundance and diversity of the wildlife. Bats, however, are New Zealand's only native land mammal.

We would be remiss in discounting the wonderful people we've met in New Zealand. In Akaroa, just under 50 miles from Christchurch on the South Island, we spoke with a local woman who related a recent story about her community. The previous week, a cruise ship disembarked 800 passengers to explore the area. When the wind picked up to the point where the ship was no longer safe in the protected bay, it was forced to move out to sea, leaving the passengers behind.

The local community immediately stepped up to house and feed them for the night. Not only is this town charming and lovely, its residents are more than gracious and welcoming.

ANTARCTICA

THERE IS NO PLACE ON EARTH LIKE ANTARCTICA, THE EARTH'S SOUTH-ernmost continent. Its remoteness, immensity, sights, and sounds are the most amazing of all the places we have visited. Although covered by ice, Antarctica is a desert which is the coldest, driest, and windiest of all the continents. The cost of travel to this remote continent combined with the rough crossing from either South America or New Zealand precludes travel for most. However, those who do visit will never forget their experience as one of the most memorable in their lifetimes. Between the two of us, we have visited Antarctica on four occasions and, should the opportunity again arise, we would be ready to return on a moment's notice!

The wildlife on the continent, most of which migrates during the frigid winters, have adapted to the barren and inhospitable landscape. Between the penguins, sea and land birds, seals, and marine creatures, there are ample opportunities to fill our memory cards.

There are no hotels, restaurants, or other trappings of civilization present on Antarctica. One either works at one of the many research stations or is a tourist who arrives by sea on a cruise or expedition ship. The tourists are off-loaded on Zodiacs or kayaks and are usually able to spend the day viewing the wildlife of the area. The

Zodiacs pick up passengers for lunch and dinner, only to drop them back onshore for evening viewings during the summer months when there is 24-hour sunlight. Watching penguins emerging from or reentering the sea, icebergs floating by with seals or birds atop, leopard or fur seals patrolling in the rough waters—or just sitting to absorb the beauty and sounds of the busy animals—are remarkable experiences.

Photographing the wildlife is a great deal of fun in Antarctica. Along with our digital cameras and lenses, we often take a small video camera to record the

movement and sounds of the activities we witness. One bright, sunny day, Shelley was filming a large group of gentoo penguins when a young, downy-furred chick approached her. The chick stood beneath her, flinging its head upwards and squawking continually, as it would do if Shelley were its mother. As Shelley had no intention of regurgitating her breakfast in response to the chick's request, the penguin finally opted to seek out another photographer for better luck.

Once when Shelley was hiking on a rocky, icy trail in Niko Harbour, located on Andvord Bay, she had the misfortune to get too close to a skua's nest, perched above on a cliff. Before she could react, the large bird, protective of its young, swept down from the cliff. Hearing a rush of air and seeing this giant bird heading for her head, she ducked in time to avoid a direct hit. Fortunately she was wearing a woolen hat which protected her head. Skuas have the reputation of being aggressive and fierce in the protection of their nests, young, and territory. Large, brown sea birds with a wingspan up to 55 inches, they are excellent fliers and are seen around penguin colonies. Although they eat primarily fish and

krill, they also supplement their diet with penguin chicks and eggs and carrion. They are often seen chasing and pestering other birds to regurgitate their meals. You quickly learn that the best way to pass through an area of skuas is with one arm extended upwards for protection.

Our adventure in this harbor did not end with the skua attack. We had been hearing ice cracking from a glacier for the three hours we'd spent wandering about the area. As it was about lunchtime, we boarded the Zodiacs for a shuttle back to our ship. We had just reached our cabin when we heard a loud, thunderous crack which turned out to be a huge calving of ice from the cliff close to the ship. We looked out the window to see a giant wave heading toward us. We immediately planted ourselves against our closet as the wave hit the side of the ship, tilting it 45 degrees. Once the wave passed, we remembered the other passengers who were still walking on land and had not made it back to the ship. Once the calving started, the people on land ran to high ground and those in Zodiacs were driven at considerable speed to the other side of the bay, behind the ship. It took close to an hour for the Zodiacs to make their way back to the ship through the thick jagged ice that covered the bay. Everyone was safe, and the stories of the calving were shared that evening and for several days thereafter.

MAINE
The Place We Call Home

OUR EXPERIENCES ON LAND AND SEA, WITH THE ENVIRONMENT, PEO-ple, and wildlife are many. Living in rural Maine on Moosehead Lake, we are able to frequently observe deer, moose, raccoons, foxes, black bears, squirrels, chipmunks, and a large variety of birds. One of our most often-related stories involves the "resident" moose, we named Margaret.

Margaret is a moose that has been coming to our yard for several years. We reside in a "no hunting" area where she has been able to live without fear of those with guns. Although, on occasion, other moose visit our salt lick, Margaret is easily identified by a large scar on her flank. Moose are large (800-1300 pounds, seven feet in height, and close to nine feet in length), awkward, and gangly in appearance, with long legs and a large, heavy nose. These beautiful animals are well-adapted to bitter cold temperatures and deep snow. We generally see Margaret and other moose in the late spring and early summer months and in late fall and early winter.

Margaret will usually return to our yard in early June, sometimes with her yearling calf or with a recently born one. This past August, during the night, Shelley awoke to noises that could not be easily identified. She rose, grabbed her flashlight, and tried to see what was making the racket outside her window. Seeing nothing, she returned to bed. When she woke the next morning, we all went to the window to see Margaret nursing her new calf. We called this new calf "Max," a generic name which, should the calf return to our yard, may be replaced once it is identified as a male or female.

❧ TALES FROM AFAR ❧

BOTH OF US HAVE WONDERFUL STORIES AND PHOTOGRAPHS FROM OUR journeys to all seven continents, but several of these stories stand out as being the most memorable. Join our adventures as we relate those tales through our photographs and recollections.

"NOISES IN THE NIGHT"
Jacklyn's Story

MY FIRST TRIP TO AFRICA WAS TO KENYA AND TANZANIA, AS IS THE case with many first-time visitors. I traveled alone and joined a group of six other women from several states. We were surprised that our group of six consisted only of women, as I would have suspected that fewer women than men would travel to Africa. Two of the six were sisters who frequently traveled together. The rest of us were strangers. But we all became friends the first day as we just "clicked." None of us had visited Africa before, so we were all in a state of heightened expectation.

We were dropped off on a dirt runway in the Maasai Mara, having left Nairobi about an hour and a half earlier on a small single-engine plane. We then boarded our safari vehicle for the trip to our first camp. The first animal we saw was a towering giraffe bending to eat the leaves of an acacia tree. The thrill of the first African animal viewed in the wild is difficult to explain. Despite an almost 24-hour series of flights with layovers and the like, and the amount of money spent on this adventure, amazingly, a new level of energy flowed through my body. On the ride from the airport, we saw so many animals and birds that we had only seen on TV or in photos that we thought we were dreaming.

Our tented camp was simple. There were eight individual tents and a thatched-roof common area where we were to meet and eat. As I am one who loves adventure but is afraid of potential dangers, I couldn't believe I was in the farthest tent from the common area, with the two sisters in the tent to my right. There were no fences around the camp, so we could only imagine what might appear around us. All was fine as we were gathered by a camp ranger to walk as a group to the dining area. After supper and campfire stories we were again lead back to our tents. By then it was dark.

We were told to remain in our tents no matter what happened or what we might hear, as we would be safe there. We were also told to zip up our canvas windows and were shown where to find a whistle, should a problem arise or assistance be required. Soon after the ranger left, the generator went off and we were in complete darkness. My imagination magnified every sound and perceived it as a predator ready to devour me in my canvas tent. I briefly turned on my flashlight, but due to my travel fatigue, I fell asleep rather quickly.

The Hyrax

Sometime during the night, a deafening screeching woke me from my dreams of dangerous predators. The sound was terrifying, and other unidentifiable screams followed. I couldn't imagine what could make such frightening sounds. As the screams continued, my perceived terror threat rose. All of a sudden, from the second tent from mine, one of the other women yelled for the entire camp to hear, "Shut the f— up!" It was so unexpected that it relieved the tension, and laughter erupted up and down the line of tents. We all started yelling back and forth to each other, questioning what we had heard. Finally the noise stopped, and after some time we fell back to sleep.

At breakfast the next morning, we continued laughing and discussing our individual reactions to that terrifying noise. When our guide appeared, he began to laugh, not at our stories but at us. He asked us to follow him, so we left our breakfast and walked to the edge of the dining area. He pointed to an animal about the size of a rabbit sitting on the roof under which we were eating. Our terrifying noisemaker was a hyrax.

The hyrax is a small furry mammal similar to a rodent, but related to elephants and manatees. These nocturnal animals graze on plant materials. They are territorial and utter unique shrieks and screams, up to 20 different calls. That night, our hyrax seemed to want to share all 20 sounds with its new tourist guests.

Lions

Just as we were adjusting to our new environment, smells, sounds, and resident East African animals, another noise elicited a new round of terror after the lights went out. Again, alone in my tent, just after retiring, I began to hear low growling, almost like the purring of large house cats. First, I thought of small domestic cats and almost immediately I envisioned CATS! My awareness of large predators that close elicited a primal fear. I picked up my flashlight and pointed it toward the origin of the sound. All I could see was a bulge where the lions appeared to be lying against my tent. I tried not to move, though I was sure my heart was beating so hard and fast that it could be heard by the animals. Should I blow my whistle for help or just sit motionless hoping that the cat or cats would get up and leave? The two sisters were again in the tent on one side of mine, and I could hear them discussing the noise. All I could do was scream silently for them to be quiet so as not to stir up the cats. I knew there was always a sentry guard, usually a Maasai warrior, who patrolled the camp day and night. The Maasai and the wild animals have an imprinted relationship of mutual respect and rarely threaten one another. As a Maasai approaches a lion, for example, the lion, respecting those humans in red with whom they are familiar, will just leave the area. Thus was the case with my cats. I heard the sentry's steps get closer and, to my surprise, the cats calmly stood and left the side of my tent. It took some time to recover from this experience, but I finally fell asleep. The next morning our guide mentioned that the sentry had reported two female lions resting against my tent the previous night, and said how relieved he was that I did not blow the whistle, as the lions might have been startled and become aggressive. I had survived another night in Africa!

Other Noises

In our many trips to Africa over the years, the nighttime noises afford the best stories. We have heard odd, unfamiliar sounds, some of which were never identified. One such night, strange new sounds came from just outside our tent. It was obvious there were a great many animals close to our canvas wall. Each of us encouraged the other to check out the strange sounds. As we gingerly unzipped the window as silently as we could, we saw a large herd of zebras pulling up and chewing vegetation just a few feet from our heads.

On another trip we had a leopard wandering between the tents for most of one night. We could hear an animal disturbing the dry vegetation beneath its feet as it walked through our camp, but were unaware of its identity until morning, when we heard the camp attendants talking about the leopard spotted the night before. We have heard chases and kills during the night, as well, and next morning, while walking to breakfast, we were we able to confirm our suspicions when we spotted bones and flesh along our path. Sometimes the sounds were easily identifiable, if our tents were located around a watering hole or along the bank of a river. One night we could barely sleep as our laughter kept us awake. For the better part of the night we listened to several hippos belching and farting as they stood in the river several yards from our tent.

"RUN!"

PREDATION IN AFRICA IS A NATURAL PHENOMENON AND PART OF THE food chain of life. When watching a chase scene on TV, we cannot get to the remote fast enough to change the channel and avoid the final moments of the terrified prey's life. In Africa, it is hard to avoid the daily struggle for survival as you travel through areas where predators and prey are always alert for a potential encounter.

We experienced our first kill several years ago on a night drive. The vehicles in areas where night drives are common are equipped with large spotlights that the ranger shines continuously from right to left to pick up either movement or the reflection in an animal's eyes. The rangers are tremendous spotters, and on one occasion ours was able to detect a four-inch chameleon on a branch 100 yards from the vehicle! Even when the chameleon was pointed out to us, we were unable to see the small reptile. Our guide then left the vehicle, walked through the brush, cut off the branch on which the chameleon was sitting, and carried it on the broken branch, back for the two us to see. After we examined the small creature, he returned it to the woods.

This one evening in Kenya after dark, we were searching for any of the larger animals that hunt during the night, like lions and leopards. We had been driving for some time, scanning left and right, when we spotted a single lioness to our right, walking slowly with head down and a creeping gait. She was obviously stalking prey, which at first we couldn't see. She was oblivious to our presence and continued to creep forward. We knew the prey was close and likewise knew that it would be unusual for a lioness to be hunting alone, but we saw neither other lions nor her prey. Finally, far in the distance, we noticed three impalas grazing in an open field. As the anticipated encounter became a reality, everyone shouted silently for the impala trio to run. The impalas were obviously upwind of the approaching lion and had no fear of the imminent attack. In a flash, the attack took place, but rather than the single lioness, six lions attacked from various directions and took down one of the impalas. Lions at night are successful hunters. As the group circles an animal, one of them drives the unsuspecting prey toward the larger group for the attack. We drove our vehicle to the scene to witness the most violent scene we can remember. The lions' attack was swift and efficient, their mouths and faces covered in blood as they ripped and tore at the carcass. As distasteful and dramatic as we found this encounter, it gave us a greater appreciation of the life-and-death struggle repeated daily in the wild. We have seen several encounters with predator and prey since, but the first was the most terrifying and memorable.

WALKING WITH LIONS

ON ONE TRIP TO CAPE TOWN, SOUTH AFRICA, WE OPTED FOR A TOUR along the Garden Route that took us northeast to a nature reserve near Mossel Bay. Our goal was to get close to and walk with lions. The experience of walking with these majestic beasts in their own African bush environment was never forgotten. After a safety briefing by the rangers, and after signing the release of liability, we met two adult lions, one large male and one younger white female. Our guides were experienced rangers who, with their long, bamboo walking sticks, strolled beside us, available should the lions exhibit aggression. We had the opportunity to follow behind these cats for about an hour with our pace determined by that of the lions. We were able to watch them interact and engage with their environment, and we were able to stop from time to time for photographs of both the lions and the beautiful scenery surrounding us.

It was only toward the end of our walk that the lions became a bit agitated and began sparring with one another. Their growls and roaring were amazing to hear at such close range. The rangers deftly separated the cats and herded the larger male away from our group. As supporters of animal conservation, we were pleased to learn that these two lions, and others in this reserve, were not the products of a breeding program but were obtained from various farms or zoos that no longer wanted or could take care of them. These lions will live on this reserve until their deaths and are thus protected from becoming hunters' prey. The ability to closely observe lions, almost as if we were part of their pack, was a thrilling and rewarding experience. The protection of these splendid animals should be a priority for all.

"WE'VE GOT A LOT TO LEARN"

ANOTHER ENCOUNTER WITH LIONS HAPPENED NEAR KRUGER NAtional Park in South Africa. We first noticed five rhinos standing in and lying around a waterhole in the distance. To the right of our vehicle, we observed three young male lions closely watching the rhinos. The lions began moving slowly toward the massive rhinos on the other side of the waterhole. Two rhinos left their group and began moving toward the area where the lions were standing. Two of the three lions seemed interested in the rhinos' approach and moved forward, while the third lion wisely stayed behind to watch the upcoming encounter. One rhino continued to advance as the two cats moved closer, until one of the rhinos stopped within a few feet of the lions.

We watched in horror in anticipation of the encounter, but rather than an immediate attack, a momentary standoff ensued. The rhinos didn't move an inch but just stared intently at the two young lions as the lions lowered their heads and began a low growl. Finally, a couple minutes later, the forward rhino dipped his head slightly, and the lions instinctively began running in panic in the opposite direction. The lions' expressions as they ran for their lives, following the small movement of the rhino, were comical. Perhaps they were not quite ready to take on such a powerful animal. The third lion met the other two, and all three fled the waterhole in anticipation of a better day in their quest to improve their hunting skills.

"TODAY, PLACE YOUR BET ON THE HYENA"

ONE OF OUR MOST UNEXPECTED OBSERVATIONS OCCURRED IN THE Ngorongoro Crater, a natural volcanic caldera located 100 miles west of Arusha in Tanzania. This crater was formed two to three million years ago, covers 100 square miles and is 2,000 feet deep. More than 25,000 animals live in the crater, and although they may leave the area, most remain. You can view lions, buffalos, zebras, rhinos, several species of antelopes, crocodiles, cheetahs, leopards, hyenas, and a large variety of birds. Of all the locations we have visited in Africa over the years, the Ngorongoro Crater is one of the most amazing places to view wildlife. As you descend into the crater, a fog bank usually obscures the treasure below. These low clouds cling to the upper rims of the crater, making the entire area appear surreal. When the vehicle ultimately clears the clouds, the expansiveness of the area is jaw-dropping, with animals spread across the crater floor as far as the eye can see. Wildebeest are chasing one another, flamingos perch on the salt bed lake, and lions are asleep in the sun. The crater is a magical place to experience and explore.

On one trip to Ngorongoro, we came upon a group of eight female lions and several adolescent cubs eating the carcass of a gazelle. We stopped to watch the behaviors of the feasting animals. One large male had eaten and had relocated about an eighth of a mile from the rest of the pride. We could see a group of perhaps 15 hyenas in the distance. With their acute sense of smell, they began to close in on the group of lions. The adult females, sensing the hyenas' approach, rose and stood guarding their young and freshly killed prey. The standoff began with neither group wishing to make the first move. We thought the "king of beasts" would use its size, strength, and reputation to dissuade other animals from approaching, but this was not the case. Apparently these lions did not get the memo!

Hyenas are very menacing looking with their lowered hind quarters, strong jaws and teeth, and nasty attitude. There are two varieties of hyena. The spotted hyenas kill up to 95 percent of what they eat, whereas the striped hyenas are largely scavengers and typically drive off larger predators, including lions.

This large cackle of spotted hyenas began stalking the lions and their prey with mock attack movements. The lions were certainly outnumbered, but our money was still on the cats to protect both their cubs and their meal. But when the hyenas got uncomfortably close, the lions thought it best to stand and gingerly walk away, always looking behind and anticipating danger. It took but a minute for the hyenas to encircle and begin to devour the abandoned carcass. All our predisposed notions about lions vanished. Perhaps the lions had about finished eating, or there were too many hyenas to put their lives and the lives of their young at risk. We will never know. We were grateful we did not observe a violent encounter and that both groups of animals survived another day.

Each time we travel to Africa, we gain new knowledge of the wildlife we observe. The guides and trackers who assist us are experienced and exceptionally knowledgeable about the environments and behaviors of the animals we see. It is such a treat to return home with new pictures and experiences to share.

"DUST CLOUDS AND CHAOS!"

W E HAVE BEEN FORTUNATE TO EXPERIENCE THE GREAT WILDEBEEST Migration in both Kenya and Tanzania on three occasions over the years. Travelers and especially photographers spend extra money to try to time the arrival of the hundreds of thousands, sometimes millions, of animals to the many camps that promote this wonderful opportunity for observing the greatest migration in the world. We have relied on luck more than money to try to catch this spectacle and have been rewarded, despite the herd arriving both earlier and later than the expected dates.

Vast numbers of migrating animal herds move through the Serengeti in an annual predictable pattern as the grazing animals follow the availability of food and water. This clockwise movement from Tanzania (Serengeti) and Kenya (Maasai Mara) is constant throughout the year and highly dependent upon rainfall.

These pictures were taken in Tanzania during two of our trips, one the last day of May and the other in early June. During the May trip, we were sitting in our vehicle watching a group of four zebras drinking from a small waterhole, when our guide spotted a dust cloud covering the horizon far in the distance. Although the migration was not expected for a few weeks, he mentioned that a distant dust cloud of that size usually portends its arrival. We had a choice of whether to go view other animals or wait at the waterhole to see if the dust cloud exposed a large group of migrating animals. Of course, we chose to wait. After we had been sitting expectantly for about 30 minutes, the dust lifted to reveal hundreds of thousands of running animals. The wildebeest and zebras were circling our vehicle on their way to the waterhole. It was complete chaos with the braying and barking of zebras, the snorting of the wildebeest, and the dust flying as agitated animals continued to arrive. The ranger said with the three merging groups of animals, there were well over a million.

The animals surrounded our vehicles, so that if we had been brazen enough, we could have reached out and touched them. There were other animals as well, including the anticipated predators awaiting the herd's arrival: impalas, Thompson gazelles, warthogs, predator birds, hyenas, jackals, and of course lions. The movement was constant and frenzied. The fear of predation was clear from the nervous pushing and shoving, as groups of animals forced their way to the waterhole. Although we watched the growing herd for close to an hour, it took us another four hours to slowly extricate ourselves from the overwhelming number of migrating animals. It was obvious that we did not need large lenses, but even the shorter lenses we took with us this day were too long for the proximity of the wildebeest, in particular. The ever-present dust cloud made it hard to breathe, and the animals' movement exacerbated the problem. We also experienced sensory overload from the smell of the animals in such close proximity. As uncomfortable as we felt with the smell and dust, we were never frightened by the enormous number of animals surrounding us.

The Great Wildebeest Migration was one of the most memorable of all our travel adventures. We will never forget our immersion in the struggle for survival or the tremendous numbers of animals that surrounded us. Exhilaration and wonderment are the two words that best reflect our experience of this stunning migration.

Each species uses camouflage to evade detection, either through its coloring, behavior, or with the assistance of others. The black and white stripes of the zebra herd make it difficult to identify a single animal. Zebra group movement becomes a blur when viewed by the predator. Zebras are also most often found around wildebeest, whose numbers offer protection. The oxpecker birds, observed on many large mammals, dine on a meal of insects and parasites, dandruff, and ear wax. The hippo and Cape buffalo, for example, may benefit from the free cleaning service provided by these birds. In addition, the birds sound an alarm call when predators are close. This symbiotic relationship is present with many animals. Monkeys also sound an alarm when predators are close, providing a warning to other animals in the area.

"YOU ARE IN THE WRONG TREE!"
Shelley's Story

THE AFRICAN BAOBAB, ALSO KNOWN AS THE "TREE OF LIFE," IS USUally portrayed as an upside-down tree with its roots pointed upward. One variety can reach heights of 150 feet and be up to 52 feet wide. The tree is ancient in its origin and estimated to have been present 200 million years ago. Baobab trees can live for thousands of years in dry and arid areas in the 32 countries where they are found. They provide food, shelter, and water for both animals and humans. The tree produces a nut (fruit) that is a rich source of vitamin C.

In northern Tanzania we were fortunate to visit a hunting and gathering people called the Hazda. Numbering under 1,000, these people, similar to the Bush People, are descendents of aboriginal hunter-gatherer tribes who have worked their land for

thousands of years. They speak with a "click" in their speech and a language that is unlike like any other. These people live in camps of 20 to 30 people in a communal setting, where the men forage for honey and still shoot game with poison arrows, and the women seek berries and baobab fruit. The baobab also serves as shelter from the weather, and the "tree of life" designation is related to the fact that the children of this tribe are born inside the hollowed-out tree.

We were lucky to have gone way into the bush to actually spend time with the Hadzabe tribe and see how they live. Since they are nomadic and don't spend a lot of time in one place, this was a real accomplishment. As we approached the area where the Hadzabe were expected to be, there was a large elephant standing in front of a massive baobab tree. Little did we know that this tree had at its base a group of men sitting and talking. When we arrived, the elephant calmly walked back into the bush. The men seemed to enjoy showing us how they hunt and also how they find and gather fruits and nuts. One interesting incident occurred when we came upon three baobab trees close together. The chief showed us where they spend time during the rainy season, inside the hollow tree. Several male members of our group

climbed into the tree to see what it was like inside. When I tried to go in, I was pushed away and told that I could not go in. The reason for this is the trees are gender-specific. Men go into one tree and the women in another. When we returned to their camp I noticed the women were in a separate area from the men. I should have known I was in the wrong tree. Although our primary mission is to photograph wildlife, these unexpected human encounters make for lasting memories as well.

"MONKEYING AROUND!"

Jacklyn's Story

EVEN DURING THE DAY, ENCOUNTERS WITH ANIMALS ARE OFTEN UN-usual and unexpected. On one trip, while I was taking a shower in an outdoor area attached to the tent, a vervet monkey decided to watch. A five-foot privacy wall surrounded the shower area. The monkey jumped from a tree branch onto the wall and sat quietly staring at me, the naked woman below. At first I was startled but then realized this animal was simply a voyeur, more than happy just to watch! Although I tried to shoo him from the wall, he chose to remain. We have had monkeys enter our tent and make off with things. On one day, a vervet monkey unzipped a canvas tent door, entered, and stole a red ball cap. The monkey was seen for the three days we remained in that camp, walking about with this red cap in hand. We never saw him with the cap on his head, but he seemed ever so proud of his newly obtained color-ful possession. We learned of another couple who lost all their medication when

a group of monkeys invaded their tent. This couple had to phone back to an American pharmacy to get replacements, a three-day ordeal. We have had monkeys take laundry, specifically underwear hanging out to dry, and parade around the camp with their new gar-ments. These vervet monkeys raid the trash bins, steal food from dining areas, and harass tourists by hanging on the safari vehicles.

The vervet monkey in this photo was quite bold in its method of obtaining break-fast. As I sat in the dining tent in Maasai Mara, I watched with concern this monkey hanging upside down from the thatched roof just be-hind me. I was startled when the vervet jumped from the roof, over my shoulder, and, with an uninterrupted motion, grabbed the breakfast roll off my plate! The monkey then crossed the table, sat in a chair across from me, and with complete confidence, ate the roll. In the photo, the food on its mouth is my breakfast! Another monkey sat across the room with another couple, picked up a cup of tea, and not only drank it as a human would, but when finished, picked up the cloth napkin to dry its lips!

Whether we are dealing with the macaques in Gibraltar, Bali, or throughout India and Indonesia, the baboons or vervet monkeys in Africa, the green monkeys of the Caribbean, or other varieties encountered on our trips around the world, we are always suspicious of what they might do next. Sometimes they are harassing, sometimes humorous, but always interesting to watch as their behaviors are so similar to the variety of human behaviors we experience in our lives. Love them or hate them, they are always entertaining.

"I'D LIKE TO MARRY YOU!"

Jacklyn's Story

IT IS ALWAYS SPECIAL TO RECEIVE A MARRIAGE PROPOSAL, ESPECIALLY from a great-looking, tall, dark, and handsome man! But I did not expect such a proposal in a remote area of the Maasai Mara in Kenya.

Our camp tents, though basic, are usually very spacious and contain an en suite, a fancy name for a private bath. Sometimes these camps are permanent and have flush toilets, and some require the camp personnel to frequently remove the contents from a sand pit below the toilet fixture (a very unpleasant arrangement for both the camp staff and the tourist). After a day on safari, I entered my tent, and after using the en suite (the flush variety), I returned to the main room to see a tall man dressed in red plaid standing inside the tent in front of the canvas door. Startled, I asked how I might help him. He replied without hesitation that he wished to marry me. I asked if we had ever met, thinking this was some prank perpetrated by other travelers with whom I had spent the day. He said, "No." When I asked him why he wanted to marry me, knowing that I was at least twice his age, he sheepishly replied that he wanted to go to America for education. When I mentioned that I was already married, he said that was no problem, as in his culture a man could have many wives. Grinning, I said that polygamy was not something that would be accepted in my country.

We chatted for close to 30 minutes about what he wanted for his family and himself, a bit about the Maasai belief that their tribe was one of the lost tribes of Israel, and his tribe's connection with nature and its wildlife. He also discussed the difficulty in reconciling older traditions and practices in a world of high-tech, speed and newer opportunities away from the rural village where he lived. Our sharing of both common and very different experiences was a wonderful exchange I will always remember. As he was leaving the tent, he asked if he could give me a gift. He removed the machete from his waist and handed it to me. The knife's sheath was worn cowhide, dyed red, and had obviously seen much use. I took the gift which today remains as a great reminder of my first personal encounter with this storied, proud, and prominent inhabitant of the Mara.

"OPEN WIDE!"

O N THE OKAVANGO DELTA IN BOTSWANA, OUR GUIDE TOOK US IN A dugout canoe to observe the animals that live in and around the water. This guide used a long bamboo pole to propel us along the lily pad-surfaced, narrow tributary. The river produced numerous birds such as the ibis, swimming and wading elephants, large crocodiles, and several other land animals drinking from its banks. As we watched a 16-foot foot crocodile on the bank, the creature slowly lifted its head and, in an instant, lunged at our canoe. When it missed, it disappeared gracefully below us. If we had been two feet closer, the croc would have landed in our boat! That close encounter raised our awareness of other threats that might lie ahead.

We continued to float forward, stopping to photograph a tiny tree frog sitting on a waxy-leafed plant whose roots extended well below the top of water. As we turned a corner, right before our canoe rose three hippos with open mouths. Unless you see bubbles atop the water, you don't know hippos are present. There have been many stories of hippos surfacing to overturn even larger boats than ours and tossing the people into the water. With crocs and hippos in these areas, the possibility of being tossed overboard was terrifying. Our guide swiftly poled our canoe backward as we snapped more photos of these large animals.

Hippos are social mammals and are often found in large groups of up to 200 animals, called bloats, schools, or pods. The hippo can weigh up to 8,000 pounds and grow to 16 feet in length and up to five feet in height. Although herbivores, they are very aggressive and dangerous, and are responsible for just under 3,000 deaths each year in Africa. They spend sixteen hours a day wallowing in the water, both to stay cool and to protect their delicate skin from the sun. Hippos do not swim but propel themselves with their large feet against objects on the water's bottom. The hippos practice their mock attacks with open mouths, grunting and crashing into one another. The hippo is able to dislocate its jaw to make it more menacing, and usually the one with the loudest and deepest grunts becomes the alpha male. As a hippo's eyes and nostrils are located on the top of their head, the animal is often seen just at the waterline. It can stay submerged for five minutes before resurfacing for air. They are very fast on land as well as in the water. Although they spend their days in the water, they leave it each night to eat and return to the waterways at dawn.

"YOU ARE GOING TO DO WHAT?"
Jacklyn's Story

O N OUR FIRST TRIP TO AFRICA, WE ARRIVED WITH PRECONCEIVED notions of what we might see and what animals we should fear. Our nervousness about threats was limited to large predators such as lions, leopards, hippos, and rhinos—and, of course, poisonous snakes. We never thought that the biggest danger would be the small inhabitants of the area we visited. We have been bitten by mosquitoes (annoying), tsetse flies (large, long house flies in appearance that bite like a bee), and a variety of other small crawling and flying insects.

One evening after a long day's safari in Tanzania, I returned to my tent, just before dusk, to shower and get ready for drinks and dinner. It is a practice of those who run the tent camps to spray for insects when cleaning the room after the safari-goers leave for the day. There was a faint smell of insecticide as I entered the tent and prepared to zip the tent flaps closed for the night. As I was pulling the zipper on one of the windows, I felt a sharp stab in the middle finger of my left hand. Instinctively, I thought I received a puncture from an acacia tree thorn. These thorns are found on trees and bushes throughout East Africa. I thought little of the prick until my hand and then my arm strangely became very painful and numb. When it continued to progress, I sought assistance from our guide, who asked if I had been bitten by an insect. I said no, as I thought it must have been a thorn. The guide and another camp steward went back to the tent to see what might have caused my injury. When they returned they indicated that a scorpion was the culprit; it was lying on the canvas floor, still alive but presumably dying from the morning spray of insecticide.

The guide said a local Maasai elder was in the dining area and would advise us on treatment. We walked to see the medicine man with the answers. Our guide described the scorpion and, after looking at my hand, knew at once that the bite was not from a poisonous variety. We had been flown and dropped off at this camp by a small plane that I hoped would not be required for medical attention, as we were far from any city or town. The shaman said he would return, as he had to retrieve something with which to extract the venom. All I saw was the machete hanging from his waist and anticipated an amputation with that weapon.

He came back about 20 minutes later with a small knife (yea!) and a shiny, black, smooth stone. He said he would make a small cut on my finger and apply the stone. Having no other alternative in the moment, I agreed to let him proceed. As my arm was still numb, I did not feel the small incision. The stone, which I have still not been able to identify, was soaked in fresh goat's milk, and when put on the open wound would adhere until the venom was ready to ooze from the open area. In about ten minutes the stone fell off my finger, a small bit of serous fluid dripped out, and the procedure was complete. The shaman said within a few hours all would be back to normal, and within two hours, the numbness and pain were gone.

I learned that the black stone came from Uganda and had been used for medicinal purposes for generations. Our guide said he saved his wife, who had been bitten on her leg by a black mamba snake while gardening. He used the stone as an interim step that provided the time he needed to get his wife to a hospital for anti-venom treatment. I knew that I had to have that stone, so bought it from him for ten dollars. I still have it, but I've been unable to identify the obsidian-like object or understand why it works. But I gained a new perspective on natural, folk, or tribal medicine and no longer discount its efficacy.

Since returning home, I learned a bit more about the medicinal stone. The black stone is also known as a snake or viper stone or as the Jerusalem stone, and is indeed used in Africa as a folk-medicine remedy for snake bites in particular. It is also used in other parts of the world including Asia and South America. These "stones" may also be carved out of animal bones or snake heads but are used in the same manner. They are also seen as protectors against evil spirits. There is no scientific evidence that these stones are effective; however, in listening to those who have reportedly used the stone successfully, and based on my own experience, they seem to be.

"CONDOS FOR RENT"

Throughout Sub-Saharan Africa, you see numerous trees with pendulum-like, beehive-shaped objects dangling from their branches.

These objects hang from the low to the highest branches and may be well over 100 in number. They are nests, often made from dried leaves, small tree fibers, twigs, and grasses. These weaver bird nests are placed in this arrangement for a few specific purposes. The more colorful males build the nests, with the most attractive garnering the interest of females. Most of these nests, especially those closest to the bases of trees, remain empty and unused as a defense against predators, especially snakes. The nests are designed and constructed by the clever birds with open holes at the bottom, making it very difficult for other predators to reach for and suspend themselves from the nest. When an African snake climbs a tree in anticipation of a meal of eggs or chicks, for example, he finds the lower nests empty and will sometimes retreat. As the snake continues to climb and finds nothing, the upper nests, holding the weaver bird eggs or chicks, remain safe from the predator. In Africa, weaver birds look very much like finches but vary in color from the yellow and black masked weaver to the black and white buffalo weaver. As with our finches, the birds are often seen in large flocks or busy entering or leaving their nests.

"WHAT IS THAT?"

IN AN ARID AREA AROUND THE HORN OF AFRICA, WE WERE FORTUNATE on a recent safari to observe two pair of gerenuks along the side of the road. These deer-like animals are quite elusive, so a sighting is always a thrill. The gerenuk, also known as the giraffe-gazelle, looks like a deer with a long, giraffe-like neck. They are very interesting in that they eat while standing on their hind legs to reach high into the trees. They are one of the few animals that require no water their entire life, as they obtain the moisture they need through the vegetation they consume; therefore, they do not need to be close to a waterhole. They live in remote areas and are very hard to locate.

The gerenuk is stunning in appearance with its shiny, smooth, red-brown coloring and beautiful facial and ear markings, especially in the female. These black and white markings and their alert posturing make these animals striking in appearance. Only the male has horns, and the male gerenuk can be seen in paintings on the ancient walls of tombs in Egypt. The gerenuks spend their day foraging, browsing, and feeding on trees and other vegetation.

"TOO CLOSE FOR COMFORT"

OUR EXPERIENCED GUIDES AND TRACKERS ARE VERY AWARE OF THE safety precautions required to avoid unnecessary encounters with animals that may prove dangerous. Many of these animals, especially in Africa, are quite territorial and protective of their young. This is especially the case when approaching a group of elephants, which can be as large as 200 animals traveling together.

Near Hwange National Park in Zimbabwe, we came across a herd of 50 or 60 elephants with juvenile and baby elephants washing, drinking, wading, and splashing water on themselves in a small waterhole. We drove off the road and sat on the opposite side of the pond watching and photographing these magnificent animals. We watched quietly for several minutes until a few of the adult elephants started to become agitated. The herd separated and began to walk closer to where our vehicle was parked. Unconvinced that we were in danger if we remained in the vehicle, and despite pleas from us to back away, our driver refused to move. We were told to just quietly sit still, and although the elephants would get close, they were not a threat. Not so!

The elephants circled our vehicle, cutting off the exit path that we needed for a quick departure. The elephants were apparently uncomfortable with our proximity to their young. They began posturing, throwing their huge ears and trunks forward, and their vocalization of anger was deafening. We knew that at any time they could overturn the vehicle. This encounter lasted for about five minutes, and as none of us moved or made any sounds (apart from silent internal screams), the elephants finally determined that we would not harm them. They began to back up, still tossing their trunks, vocalizing, and scratching the ground. The herd finally cleared away from our vehicle so we could breathe again. We learned that a few weeks earlier in another park, a group of elephants did overturn a vehicle and trampled one of its occupants. There is a time when safety must take precedence over the perfect shot. We were so disturbed by our driver's disregard for our safety that we promptly reported his actions. He no longer is permitted to guide others in this area.

"ONE IN FIFTY"

PHOTOGRAPHING BIRDS CAN BE CHALLENGING, ESPECIALLY WHEN USing large, heavy telephoto lenses. You learn pretty quickly that trying to chase a bird in flight is impossible, but if you anticipate the flight path, your photo hopefully will capture the bird mid-flight with a pre-focused lens and a fast speed adjustment to avoid a blurry or out-of-focus shot. If you observe an unattended nest with young chicks or eggs, patience is the attribute needed as you await the nesting bird's return.

It is not always possible to prepare your camera settings in advance for an unexpected situation with animals in the wild. Such was the case with this spontaneous shot of an Egyptian goose taken in Zambia. While walking along a river bank,

we spotted a group of perhaps fifty tan-colored geese standing in an area about 25 yards ahead. As we have many shots of these birds, we lowered our cameras seeking another subject to photograph. Unexpectedly, the flock of birds took flight, and in the midst of the mass of tan and gray birds was a single bird with beautiful plumage. The bird's white, teal, and reddish feathers perfectly picked up the light from above. Raising our cameras hastily, we had only time to set the shutter speed and caught this Egyptian Goose mid-flight. The other photographers did the same, and the sound of several cameras' rapid-fire shutter speed clicks was quite humorous. This was not the only image we captured but one of about 50 that we each took. Thanks to digital photography, we were able to delete almost all the other photos in which the bird was out of focus, partially out of the frame, or missed altogether. Fortunately, this particular image of the bird in flight was captured as if we had prepared for the "perfect shot." Luck plays an important role, both in your ability to find birds and animals, and in whether or not the shot is successful.

"HAPPY FEET"

SOMETIMES IN AFRICA THE SMALLEST CREATURES CAN BE JUST AS IN-teresting as the larger ones. When driving on bumpy dirt roads, covered in dung from a variety of animals and footprints from numerous others, you may notice a very industrious insect, the dung beetle. We always ask our driver to stop so we can observe the large, black insects running their feet over the fresh elephant droppings like lumberjacks in the log-rolling contest at a summer fair. The male beetles roll the dung into a variety of different-sized balls, which grow as their footwork continues. If the beetle falls off, it deftly hops back on to continue rolling. Another group of dung beetles is charged with digging the tunnels to accommodate the dung balls, and a third type doesn't roll or tunnel but resides in the manure. This interesting insect can be over an inch in length. Its amazing strength is evidenced by the fact that it can bury a ball of dung 250 times its weight in a single night.

These dung balls are used for two purposes. First, the dung beetle uses it as a food source. Second, these balls are used as breeding chambers in which eggs are laid, and the hollow mass of dung then becomes food for the young beetles. Another interesting fact about these insects is that they are the only non-human animal to use the Milky Way for navigation. They are found on all continents except Antarctica.

"WE ARE ALL GOING TO DIE!"

Traveling to Antarctica on a small expedition ship, even on a good day, is always a challenge. Whether you begin the journey from Christchurch, New Zealand, from Ushuaia, Argentina, or from Punta Arenas, Chile, sailing through the churning seas makes you wonder why you wanted to do this in the first place. The weather plays a huge role in the comfort of the crossings to the world's most remote continent. When traveling from South America, ships must transverse 600 miles of the Drake Passage, at the confluence of the Atlantic, Pacific, and Southern Oceans. Our third trip was the most memorable in terms of weather, with high winds and waves pounding the small icebreaker.

We left Ushuaia in the late afternoon in January for our first stop in the Falkland Islands, where we visited several colonies of Rockhopper, Magellanic and King penguins, seals, and loads of sea and land birds. Our woes began after we left Stanley on our voyage south toward the Orkneys, South Shetland, and South Georgia. We passed through the Southern and Antarctic Ocean currents that continuously circle around the Antarctic continent. The names given to the longitudinal lines, which include the Roaring 40s, the Furious 50s, and the Screaming 60s, give some indication of the problems that may arise en route.

The winds continued to rise to Beaufort scale 11, and the waves and swells crashed against the hull and over the bow and bridge. The dark ocean color turned turquoise as the waves swept over the bridge. It was very difficult to walk through the halls of the icebreaker as it pitched and rolled. Just as we would set our feet to be ready for the next swell, the ship would move in a different direction. The icebreaker we were on had been used by the Russian Navy prior to being purchased for tourist visits to the Polar Regions. It was small, carrying fewer than 100 passengers, and had little common space, a small galley, and narrow, dark hallways. The cabins were also quite small with a shared side table between twin beds, a small closet for each bed, and a modest bathroom.

As the seas continued to rise, lines were tied around the larger common rooms so passengers could hold on as we tried to walk about the ship. Its rounded bottom makes an icebreaker very unstable in open water, but as it reaches the ice, its bow is thrust atop the ice, and its weight cracks the ice below to allow passage. The corkscrewing motion of an unstable ship as it rises to meet 30- to 40-foot waves and swells and then rocks and pitches as it descends the wave is an experience I hope to never repeat. The only time we were not being hurled about the ship was when we were able to duck into an island bay at night. Even on land, the wind made it difficult to hold a camera steady.

We experienced katabatic winds on two occasions. We usually had a few minutes to prepare, as we would first see a large menacing cloud of snow and ice appear on the horizon and atop a mountain crest. On both occasions, the ship's horn was sounded, and we were asked to return to the ship at once, to avoid being caught in the maelstrom of dangerous weather about to engulf us. On one occasion we barely made it onboard, thanks to our Zodiac diver gunning the engine. There were about 20 passengers who were unable to board their Zodiacs in time and were left on the beach to find shelter wherever they could behind boulders or vegetation. These katabatic winds come up quickly, are very powerful, and produce blinding blizzards. The ship, having pulled out of the bay for safety, returned about an hour later to retrieve the wet, cold, and frightened passengers who had been left behind.

Despite the horrific weather and seas, this trip was one of our best from a wildlife photography perspective. We obtained wonderful images of many of the permanent and seasonal inhabitants of the region, from a variety of penguins and other sea birds to seals, whales, and the most pristine and beautiful icebergs we had ever seen. The isolation and beauty of the continent stretched our imagination and overloaded our senses.

The icebreaker, on the other hand, was heavily damaged by the combination of waves and winds. While on the open sea, cabinet doors had been ripped from their hinges and furniture strewn around the common spaces. A ten-foot sofa, bolted to a hardwood floor, had been dislodged with big chunks of the floor still attached. Our cell phones, stored in our purses inside suitcases in the cabin closet, were shattered. There was not much left of the interior of the ship. We had great difficulty returning to Argentina and were low on food when we arrived. We spent most of our sea time standing on the bridge so we could watch the horizon and the waves washing over it. Although the beginning of the trip was more of an adventure, toward the end of our six-week voyage, we were in real danger. Most passengers and some of the crew were seasick much of the time. We wondered whether we would survive our experience. After our terrifying voyage to Antarctica, the icebreaker was retired and reduced to salvage. Although our other trips to this region were frequently rough and not always pleasant, the fear of death only surfaced on this trip. But once we got home, all we could talk about was how and when we could return! Antarctica is the most magically remote area in the world, and a photographer's dream.

"THERE ARE TOO MANY TO COUNT!"

ONCE YOU RECOVER FROM AN EXCITING CROSSING FROM SOUTH America to the Falklands or from New Zealand's Sub-Antarctic islands to Antarctica, the prime objective of the often difficult voyage is to see penguins. There are six types of penguins on this continent. You will find the King penguin to the north, living mostly on land, and the Emperor to the south, living on the ice. Even in the Falklands there are more penguins than you can imagine.

The first time we spotted a penguin in the wild was on the Falkland Islands where, after disembarking from the expedition ship, the Zodiac shuttle landed us on a desolate beach where an old derelict whaling ship lay. There were a few caracara, skua, and seagulls walking along the beach, but there were no penguins to be seen. We began walking up along a sandy path, wondering whether we would ever see the promised penguins. As we continued upward, we became aware of an unfamiliar odor and heard bird sounds ahead. When we finally reached the crest of the hill, the landscape opened to expose thousands of rockhopper penguins nesting or bounding about. There were

albatross circling above, and the sounds and smells of this wonderful ridge was breathtaking. We didn't know where to focus our cameras, and since it was in pre-digital days, we frequently had to stop to change rolls of film! We didn't need longer lenses, as the birds were right in front of us. This first sighting will always be special.

The tiny, adorable rockhopper penguins are found on rocky cliffs. Some were bounding from one rock to another, while long lines of others were on the way to the water far below or swimming through the strong currents that splash the rocks at the edge of the coast as they attempted to return to their nests. These birds build their nests among those of the brown-browed albatross. This interspersing of nests is quite remarkable, and results in continuous frantic movement. You can get quite close to these birds, and a few might walk up to tourists for even closer shots. The rockhoppers are small crested birds with red eyes, white bellies, and black bodies. They have pink webbed feet and spiky, sharp feathers. These birds are seen not only in the Falklands but in other Sub-Antarctic islands as well.

The Magellanic penguin of the Falklands is quite different. You must move to the side as long lines of these birds emerge from or return to the sea in a steady stream

of waddling movement. They are small-to medium-sized birds with white fronts, black backs, a white swirl about the head and another that runs to the back of their bellies and breasts. They have a large, black, bulbous beak and sound more like braying donkeys than penguins. Unlike the rock-hopper that nests on rocky cliffs, the Magellanic penguin burrows in the sand or under bushes. When you walk around these sand dune caves, the penguins poke their heads out of their burrows to watch you walking by. Magellanic penguins are also seen in places like Magdalena Island near Punta Arenas in Chile, and in Argentina. The Magellanic is similar to the African penguin and is migratory.

King penguins show very different behaviors and nesting choices. They also can be seen in great numbers entering and exiting the sea but usually do not do so in big groups. They are found in the Sub-Antarctic Islands, Antarctica, and also on the Falkland Islands where a smaller colony resides. You can see millions of them in such areas as Salisbury Plain, St. Andrews Bay, or Gold Harbour on South Georgia Island. There are also major colonies on Macquarie Island.

King penguins do not build nests but stand patiently with an egg atop their feet for up to 55 days, swapping parental duties every six to 18 days. When one parent returns from the sea, a role reversal takes place. This behavior continues until the chick hatches. Once the chick is free of the egg, the parents continue alternating care for an additional 30 to 40 days to feed their young. It is at this time that the young chick is in danger of predation from the large skuas, which will swoop down from the sky to snatch up any unprotected chick. Huge groups of adults stand together with their young. While one adult parent is out to sea fishing, the other remains with the chick. Older chicks stand in crèche-like groups, like children at recess in a schoolyard. They too await the return of a parent with food, and despite the hundreds of thousands of birds in an area, the calls of the parent and chick are specific to those birds. The parent and chick are able to find one another amidst the cacophony of sounds with their individualized vocalization.

These older chicks have thick brown coats of fur. Until this fur is shed, the young penguin is not insulated against the cold and cannot enter the sea to feed. The chick must still rely on the parents to regurgitate their catch deep into its mouth for 30 days or more. As the young penguin is fledging, it begins losing its fur in patches and clumps. These birds walk about, shaking and looking hilarious in odd outfits of downy fur randomly molting from their bodies. Some have partial coats still present, and others have tufts of fur hanging from their feathered underbodies in odd arrangements. As the chicks get older and a bit braver, they begin to approach tourists, whether we are standing, walking, or just sitting on the ground. They sometimes will walk across

our outstretched legs, inspect our boots, or stand below us squawking for food.

There are usually a large number of feisty fur seals, both adults and young, lying about in the tussock grass mounds or walking on the beach. They must be carefully watched, as they will attack the unobservant tourist should one come close. We usually take a walking stick when we disembark, in order to ward off these sometimes aggressive seals. The young seals and penguins often challenge one another in mock battles. As a group of several young penguins approaches close to a young fur seal, the seal will practice his moves and cause the penguins to waddle away as fast as they are able. This behavior goes on for hours and is quite amusing for those of us walking along the beach.

One of the most enjoyable penguins to watch is the Gentoo with its black back feathers, white front, and a swatch of white above the eyes.

They live on bleak beaches on the Falklands, South Shetland Islands, and the Antarctic Peninsula, where they build circular nests made of small stones. Much of their day involves gathering more stones and reinforcing their simple nests. This reinforcement is continual, as the most commonly observed behavior is the thievery that occurs between the birds and their neighbor's nest. These nests are separated only by the distance between the birds' outstretched flippers. When one bird turns its back, the neighboring birds rush to the unattended nest and steal stones which they take back to their pile. Sometimes a bird remains in the nest but is inattentive, so there is much flapping, pecking, and protective behavior if another brazen bird attempts to steal a stone. We could only laugh at these raids, because when the thief's nest is similarly left unattended, the offended bird returns the favor by stealing a stone back. This behavior is continuous, and at any moment in time you can see multiple birds lifting stones from others' nests and scurrying back to their own.

One of the most distinctive penguins, and one of our favorites, is the Chinstrap. This medium-sized black and white bird is one of only two types of penguins with a white face (the other being the royal). The black cap and the strap running under its chin give it a comical appearance. It breeds in large colonies on rocky slopes. The Chinstrap penguin can be found from the Antarctic Peninsula northwards including the Sub-Antarctic islands. As we approach our landing sites, the brash vocalizations of the Chinstrap penguins are the first indication that an unbelievable scene will present itself when we land.

The Macaroni penguin is a crested penguin that is known to be quite feisty and is found on South Georgia and other islands as well as Antarctica. They are social penguins that spend most of their time at sea searching for food. These birds are also black

and white with pink feet and red eyes. Although they are the most numerous of the penguins, they are a challenge to view and photograph, as they live on rocky, hilly slopes in difficult areas to reach. It is said that the name "Macaroni" was given to them by British explorers who noticed their yellow crested feathers were similar to hats worn by those at home called macaronis. Our song, "Yankee Doodle Dandy," also references these feathers.

As you move down to the continent's peninsula, the Adelie penguin is the primary bird you see. This small black and white bird with black eyes encircled by a white ring is found amid the ice floes and can be seen entering and leaving the sea in large groups. Often predator seals, especially the leopard seal, patrol close to shore. The penguins are acutely aware of the danger and stand on the water's edge awaiting the arrival of others before entering the sea. With a large group entering at one time, there is less likelihood of a single bird being caught by a seal. The same behavior in waiting for other birds to amass occurs as the penguins prepare to emerge from the ice-covered water. From the shore, you can stand and watch as the group of swimming penguins gets larger and larger until the grand exit occurs as the group, in apparent panic, speed-swim to the shore.

From time to time you see a leopard seal not far from shore with a black and white bird in its mouth. But the penguins' survival strategies work for the majority of birds, as most enter and emerge from the sea unscathed. The Adelie penguins are only found in Antarctica and are loud and feisty. They build their nests on stones separated by the distance of two penguins with outstretched flippers. Their rookeries are large and sometimes contain more than 250,000 pairs. They are often seen swimming across the ice on their bellies with their flippers acting as oars, pushing them along.

The Emperor is the largest of the penguin family, standing four feet in height and weighing up to 100 pounds. They can usually be found on pack or shelf ice between the 66th and 77th degree south latitudes of the continent. Their story has been told many times in documentary films, as they

remain on the continent year round, including the most brutal winters on the planet. These birds do build nests, but once an egg is laid, it remains atop the male parent's feet, protected by an abdominal skin fold, for up to four months while the female is at sea feeding. The male may have fasted for up to 115 days before his mate returns. The males care for the egg throughout the frigid winter, huddled together with their backs to the wind in large groups. The group continually rotates, with those penguins exposed to the elements moving to the middle of the group to conserve heat.

We would be remiss if we didn't specifically mention the leopard seal (sea leopard) that lurks in the sea around penguin and bird colonies. It is second in size to the elephant seal and second only to the orca (killer whale) as a predator. This large seal is earless, muscular, and dark in color with spots. It can be as large as 12 feet in length and weigh up to 1,300 pounds, and it preys on penguins and their chicks as well as other seabirds and fish. It will grab a penguin by the feet and fling it back and forth on the surface of the water to kill the unsuspecting sea bird. We often see this predator on the ice grabbing a penguin off the shore.

The danger for penguins never ceases whether they are swimming or on land. Skuas swoop from the air to snatch young chicks on land, and predators like seals and orcas attack from the sea. The severe weather in and around the Southern Ocean, the lack of fish which necessitates long swims for food, and other environmental dangers are always present. Penguins must be respected as tough little birds where survival is their life. Given the opportunity to return to Antarctica, our decision would be a clear "any time!"

"WHAT IS WRONG WITH THIS PICTURE?"

ONE OF OUR MOST UNUSUAL PHOTOGRAPHS, AND ONE FREQUENTLY used by teachers in their classes, is one of penguins and reindeer in the same shot. This picture was not altered. We were taught in school that Northern and Southern Hemisphere animals never met in the wild. You see the polar bear, reindeer, and walrus in the north and penguins in the south. Attempts have been made to relocate the animals to the opposite hemisphere, but they have always failed.

This photograph was taken on the Sub-Antarctic island of South Georgia. We expected to see penguins here, but the appearance of reindeer was a real shocker. The reindeer are a legacy from the time the Norwegian whalers worked this area in the early twentieth century. Reindeer, suited for both arctic and sub-arctic environments, were brought with the whalers

from the north for food. When whaling was stopped in 1967 and the area vacated, the reindeer were left behind. As grazers, they found enough vegetation to sustain them, and as penguins eat krill and small fish, there was no competition for food. This unusual cohabitation worked well for both species, and both were doing well until recently. Since our visit, the numbers of reindeer have exceeded the number that can successfully thrive, so efforts have been made of late to eradicate these wonderful animals. We were fortunate to see this combination on our last trip to Antarctica, and although we'd heard that we might see these animals together, we were more than pleased when a small group of reindeer appeared while we were photographing the King penguins. They were quite calm and did not mind us walking around them. Whether this unusual observation will be possible in the future is unknown.

"THIS PICTURE HAS NOT BEEN PHOTOSHOPPED!"

ANOTHER FAVORITE PHOTO OF OURS, AND ONE OFTEN REQUESTED ON either canvas or high-definition metal, is this one of a large elephant seal framed by King penguins taken on South Georgia Island. After disembarking on Zodiacs from the expedition ship, we are usually able to spend several hours or an entire day wandering around or sitting and observing the huge numbers of animals, including a variety of penguins, other sea birds, and large numbers of seals carrying on their daily routines. We enjoy the sensory overload, not only the sights, but also the vocalization of the various birds and seals and the smell of fresh guano covering the ground.

Huge, earless elephant seals can be seen lying along the shore, belching and passing gas. The males of this species can reach up to 20 feet in length and weigh 4,000 pounds. You see these large animals violently hurling their mass at one another, jockeying for beach rights as the alpha male, as the younger seals practice their posturing for dominance. There is much grunting and roaring, and usually the seal making the deepest and loudest noise is perceived as the strongest and will oversee the harem of 40 to 50 females. The loser of these battles must find another territory.

We were fortunate enough to capture this image of an elephant seal sitting proudly in front of numerous adult King penguins. You can also see some youngsters

in their brown fur enjoying the warmth of the sun. These young penguins must remain on land and be fed by their parents until they completely shed their fur. They are unable to swim until white and black feathers replace this blanket of down, as the fluffy fur does not provide insulation for the chicks.

The King penguin is a tall, erect, and regal-appearing bird who returns from the sea looking shiny white and clean, which is not the case with other penguins These are the second-largest variety, smaller only than the Emperor penguin that lives farther to the south. The King penguin is identified by its colorful yellow and orange markings at the beak and breast and the swath of color about the head and neck. The juveniles are wooly, fluffy brown and very comical to view and photograph. As they mature and become ready to enter the sea, you can observe these young penguins in various stages of losing their down, while their true black and white feathers appear below.

"ANYONE WANT TO SEE THE WHALES?"

Tourists visit Antarctica in its summer months after the ice melts and before winter returns. Tours to that continent generally are offered between November and March each year. If you travel in November, you see a lot of activity related to nest building as well as eggs or the hatching of penguin chicks. If you tour in the months of January and February, the penguins are fledging and are about to begin their lives fishing in the sea. We prefer not to travel in March, when a second hatching of chicks may arrive too late to survive and are often left behind as the parents migrate to warmer areas in anticipation of the coming winter. It is difficult to watch dead and dying birds being exploited by predators, so we much prefer the earlier months.

The small expedition ship or icebreaker is the best way to explore the animal-rich areas, as you can disembark and walk among the animals in their own environment, and experience the behaviors of those adorable creatures. Large cruise ships "drive by" the icebergs to view a few penguins and birds, but as they do not stop, their passengers are unable to leave the ship and experience what it is really like for animals that live in this isolated region of the world.

During the late spring and summer months in Antarctica, it is never totally dark. The sun may dim for an hour or two, but for the most part, you can remain in exploration mode well into the night. Once such evening about 11 o'clock, the ship's crew made an announcement that there were several humpback whales close to the ship and offered to deploy kayaks and Zodiacs for anyone wishing to disembark. Not willing to miss an opportunity to get close to these massive creatures, and despite our fatigue from walking and photographing penguins and seals for most of the day, we dressed and left the ship. As we wanted to take close-up photos of the whales, we took our longer lenses.

It did not take long for two whales to come up to our vessel. A mother and calf approached our kayak and dove beneath it. The water is crystal clear in Antarctica, and you can see hundreds of feet below the surface when the seas are calm, as they were in the bay where the ship was moored. The bay was dotted with small and large icebergs in varying shapes and sizes. The scene was surreal with wonderful lighting as the sun lowered, leaving an ethereal reflection of icebergs on the surface of the water. The two whales suddenly surfaced on the other side of the kayak. This spy-hopping behavior was repeated for close to 45 minutes with the two whales gently diving and surfacing from one side of our boat to the other with nary a ripple on the surface, either when they dove or when they resurfaced. We were able to reach out and stroke the whales, which seemed more interested in playing and observing us than in fearing us or leaving the area. Two other groups of photographers had similar experiences.

Our biggest problem for us was that we only brought 300mm lenses, which were much too long given the proximity of the animals. Our disappointment and self-recrimination for not bringing other lenses failed to lessen our thrill at this unbelievable encounter. For a brief outing in a small Zodiac or kayak, we try to carry as little as we can, as we don't want sea water, which will usually pool at the bottom of the vessel, to damage our equipment. The problem was that we had no photos! As we climbed back aboard the ship, we couldn't hide our chagrin. We vowed to never repeat this short-sighted decision to anticipate what lens would do the trick.

When we arrived for breakfast the next morning, a couple of other passengers joined our table, and after exchanging pleasantries, we learned that they too had taken the opportunity to play with the whales the previous evening. When we leave the ship in the chilly air, everyone looks alike in their red hooded parkas, so it wasn't unusual that we'd not observed these two fellow photographers outside the ship. Much to our surprise and delight, we learned that one of the men had close to 45 minutes of video of us with our sea mammal encounter! They told us they would send us a copy when they returned home. We cherish this video and are delighted to share it with those who appreciate our good fortune to have experienced the unbelievable.

"WHAT AM I?"

WHILE VISITING A NATIONAL NATURE RESERVE IN BARBADOS, WE came upon an animal that we had never seen before, which appeared to be a cross between a deer and a rabbit. The mara, the world's fourth largest rodent, stands 18 inches tall and has a face like a rabbit with the body and legs of a squat deer. Like a rabbit, the mara has long ears, a stocky body, and hind legs are longer than those in front. This animal is related to the guinea pig and is found in the Patagonia region of Argentina. Like a deer, the mara has hoof-like feet with three clawed digits on the hind ones and four on the front. It hops and bounces on all four feet and can jump six feet in the air. One unusual thing about the mara is that it can change from being nocturnal to diurnal and has been successfully raised by humans. It forages for fruits, vegetables, and other low vegetation.

"RATS AND BUGS, OH MY!"
Jacklyn's Story

WHILE TRAVELING THROUGH AND VISITING THE PERUVIAN AMAzon basin on rivers and small tributaries, we were struck by the lush and colorful vegetation, the numerous birds, and the large neon blue butterflies flitting past our canoe. As beautiful as the view was above, we were also aware of the dangerous creatures living below, such as the caiman and other crocodiles as well as piranhas awaiting their next meal. When the first silver fish jumped into our canoe and landed on my lap, my mind immediately identified it as a piranha. In only took a few seconds for me to grab the squirming fish and fling it out of the vessel. Our guide, laughing at my naiveté, explained that the fish was not a piranha but another small fish common in the waters that posed no threat.

The prevalent color you see is green, with as many shades as you can imagine. The water is dark and often brownish in color.

We moved deeper into the jungle, silently passing protruding branches within the mass of dense trees and hoping that our guide's knowledge of the river was absolute. As the corridors narrowed and our sense of claustrophobia rose, we could appreciate the imagined dangers. Our journey remained silent except for the continual buzzing of insects and the steady splash of the oars as we moved forward. When the river started to widen again, we began to see small groups of people fishing, bathing, or doing laundry in the water, some waving and some wary of our approach. We repeated this journey each day and were able to stop from time to time to visit a local tribe's village and learn about their culture, traditions, hardships, and joys.

We usually stayed in small, modest cottages with thatched roofs and had to walk through trees and bushes on a narrow dirt walkway to and from the river to our accommodation and a central area for meals. Our imaginations ran wild at the thought of possible threats watching us from behind the bushes. Insects, even in the cottages were problematic.

One morning we arose to thousands of small crawling insects in our beds and under the bed sheets and pillows. A steady stream of these small critters formed long lines, emerging from a small crack under the door, along the floor and up the bed frame. Before we retire, we always check our accommodations thoroughly for any hiding bugs, insects, or snakes. The room had been clear the night before. We even blocked the bottom of the door with a towel to dissuade anything from entering our space. Obviously, that action had no effect on the marching lines of insects.

Another morning, just before daybreak, we rose and started to walk toward the dining area when we heard a rustling of leaves to our left. We stopped suddenly, wondering what would appear. From behind the bushes lining the path, a large brown animal walked out just in front of us. It looked like a giant rat! It didn't seem threatening and, in fact, didn't seem to notice we were there. Ignoring us, it appeared to be on a preplanned mission as it made a left turn and started walking toward the dining area. We followed it at a safe distance.

When the animal reached the wooden steps to the building, it did not hesitate but calmly climbed with purpose, pushed open the screen door, and entered. It approached one of the dining tables like a dog awaiting scraps and just stood staring at the startled tourists until the camp staff escorted it from the dining table, down the stairs, and back to the wild. Apparently it tried this maneuver frequently.

We learned that the animal was a capybara, the largest rodent in the world, closely related to the guinea pig. They are native to South America and live in dense forests in groups that may reach 100 animals. The capybara can reach up to 200 pounds and grow to be two feet high. These semi-aquatic mammals are herbivores and are included in the diet of the anaconda.

These unexpected types of encounters with both large and small animals in the wild are always exciting additions to our travels. Although we may be startled at first, we are always able to appreciate our good fortune to be able to view the diversity of the wildlife that inhabits parts of the world that most people never see.

"DARWIN AND THE BLUE FEET"

HAVE YOU BEEN TO THE GALÁPAGOS? THIS DESTINATION IS THE ONE people most ask us about. The animals photographed there often take a back seat to the big five animals that reside in Africa, but those viewed in the Ecuadoran Galápagos are just as fascinating to observe and learn about.

Galápagos is a marine reserve and UNESCO World Heritage Site located just over 550 miles east of Ecuador off the South American continent. The 18 main and three smaller island archipelagos rise from the Pacific Ocean, cross the equator, and consist of many different ecosystems. As this is a private and protected nature reserve, you must travel with a licensed tour operator, usually on a small expedition ship, to hop on and off some of the most interesting islands in the world.

Charles Darwin explored, mapped, and documented his visit in journals, and his artist companion, John Gould, provided hand-drawn images of the previously unknown animals and plants they found. There are many varieties of birds including the blue-eyed cormorant and Darwin finch, crustaceans like the Sally Lightfoot crab, and reptiles such as land and marine iguanas, tortoises, and penguins. One of the most requested inhabitants to view and photograph are the blue-footed boobies, although there are also red-footed varieties which are more difficult to spot.

The blue-footed booby, a fairly large white-fronted and brown-winged bird with a thick bill, is easily recognizable by its bright turquoise feet. It lives in tropical and subtropical areas, including the Galápagos, and has a wingspan of three feet. The boobies dive and swim in groups for small fish such as sardines, anchovies, and flying fish, and generally eat their prey while underwater. An interesting fact about their reproductive cycle is that hatching of their one to three eggs occurs all at once, so with the variation in chick size, there is often infanticide or siblicide when food is scarce.

The marine iguanas are some of our favorite residents to watch and photograph. These reptiles are dark in color, two to three feet in length, and are either seen in large groups sitting on the rocky beaches enjoying the sun or can be observed entering the water or emerging from the sea with big chunks of sea salt clinging to their faces and bodies. They are able to dive more than thirty feet. Land iguanas, found in the desert-like areas, are more yellow and orange in color and can be seen walking about eating cacti and other arid plants, or basking in the sun on volcanic rocks. The prickly-pear

cactus makes up most of their diet, and as rain is scarce on the islands for much of the year, they also utilize the moisture in the plants. They sleep at night in burrows to conserve their body heat. These iguanas are two of many species of animals found only on the Galápagos Islands.

The Galápagos tortoises are the largest in the world, reaching 900 pounds. They are found on seven of the islands and vary in shell shape and size, depending on the humidity or aridity of the environment. They forage much of the day and bask in the sun just after dawn to absorb its heat. On the larger islands, the tortoises migrate from sea level to higher elevations in the dry season and are known to travel the same routes, known as "tortoise highways," as they have for generations.

One of the most interesting stories about a specific giant tortoise is the one about Harriet. This tortoise was brought from the Galápagos during Charles Darwin's 1835 voyage of the *HMS Beagle*, when the she was the size of a dinner plate. Harriet was estimated to be 175 years old when she died at the Australia Zoo in 2006. She lived her last twenty years under the watch of Steve Irwin and his family who acquired her in 1987. Over a period of almost 200 years, it was quite a coincidence that Harriet became the link between Darwin and Steve Irwin. Also interesting is the fact that Harriet and Steve Irwin died the same year.

"THAT IS A HUGE LIZARD!"

WE WERE ABLE TO VIEW THE KOMODO DRAGON ON THE INDONESIAN Island of Komodo, located in the Indonesian island chain northwest of Australia. The komodo is the largest of the monitor lizard family and can grow to a length of ten feet and weigh up to 200 pounds. As they have no predators, they dominate the islands where they live. The Komodo dragon is a carnivore and hunts birds and mammals, including deer, but also will seek out carrion. The animal has a long, yellow, forked tongue and a tail as long as its body. Its skin has armored scales. Its tongue has both sensory and taste receptors, and by swinging its head from side to side as it moves, it may be able to better seek out its prey.

The Komodo dragon can take down a deer and kill the animal with its sharp teeth and claws. If the animal happens to escape, the dragon also has a venomous bite that acts as an anticoagulant and causes a drop in blood pressure, paralysis, and eventual loss of consciousness. The incapacitated animal will die, sometimes over a period of days. Komodo dragons may be aggressive and have been known to attack humans, so a visit to their territory carries with it a bit of risk.

After disembarking from our ship and receiving a briefing on the Komodo dragon and safety precautions, we began our trek on a narrow path through a forested area. We had three guides with long walking sticks leading and following our group as we moved deeper into the island, intently watching for any movement in the brush. We finally reached an opening where we spotted four dragons resting in the sun. They seemed not to pay attention to our camera clicks or conversations. When we left this grouping, we walked a bit farther and spotted two more

Komodo dragons, a wild boar coming from behind the bushes, and several small deer, apparently unaware of the proximity of dragons. We were never truly frightened by our walk through the dragons' domain, despite the real and imagined dangers.

"THERE'S BLOOD IN THE WATER!"

WHILE OPEN-WATER SNORKELING THE AREA OF CABO SAN LUCAS off the Mexican coast, where the Pacific Ocean and Sea of Cortez meet, we were excited to encounter a herd of approximately 50 large sea lions frolicking and swimming close to a reef about 75 yards from us. For several minutes they seemed not to notice us and continued to play in the surf as the water crashed onto the reef. One of the seals spotted our group and apparently sounded an alarm that there were humans nearby. Within a second or two, all of the seals started swimming toward us at breakneck speed. The sea lions appeared especially menacing as we were viewing their approach through a dive mask with a magnifying lens. All we could see were huge eyes, whiskers, and teeth flying at us. The animals began bumping into us, rolling onto our backs, pushing us underwater, and disrupting our attempts to breathe through our snorkels. It was a frightening situation as their play became a threat to our safety. They did not intend to harm us, but we were uneasy with both the size and the number of the sea mammals.

When we looked to the right we saw a stream of blood flowing from one of the swimmer's thighs, and our immediate reaction was fear that sharks would smell

the blood and appear. Apparently, during one of the bumping encounters, one of the seals took a nip from the swimmer's leg through the wetsuit, probably by accident. The fear of sharks is a common one, and the perceived threat elicited a primal fear reaction from all of us. We couldn't get back to the ship fast enough. The seals' play continued as they rolled against our backs while we attempted to swim, and persisted in bumping into us from below. We weren't sure what was hitting us from underneath, and the fear of a shark attack propelled us to swim as fast as we could. It was a great relief to be pulled into the boat, grateful to have made it safely without further incident. Since that encounter, we have been very hesitant to experience open water swimming again. The potential dangers will keep us in shallow waters in the future.

"GET BACK TO THE SHIP!"

IT IS MUCH EASIER TO VISIT ANTARCTICA AND PHOTOGRAPH PENGUINS than to go to the Arctic region to obtain images of polar bears and walrus. Penguins return to the same area each year to lay eggs and raise their young, so the expedition ships know where to spot those animals and deploy the kayaks and Zodiacs for passengers to disembark. You can walk or sit with penguins and seals without safety concerns. In the Arctic, however, the ships are continually sailing in and between ice floes in search of the elusive and solitary polar bears. It is a 24-hour-a-day proposition with the crew standing ready throughout the day and night in hope of seeing a bear. The bears are almost the same color as the ice, are solitary unless you see a female with up to three cubs, and are very difficult to spot. In the case of walrus, these large animals also may be anywhere, either sitting in large groups along the coastline or floating by on a moving ice floe. The photos here were taken around Svalbard, an island off the coast of northern Norway, far above the Arctic Circle.

The crews of the small expedition ships stand watch day and night with passengers and photographers assisting. Large lenses on tripods line the observation decks. If a bear is spotted at any time (it remains light at night in this region), the ship is maneuvered to bring it as close as possible. During the first few nights of the expedition, whenever we were awakened by the captain via an intercom in the cabin, we all shed our nightclothes, got dressed, put on our parkas, grabbed our camera equipment and ran to an outer deck to view the bear. By the third or fourth night, no one bothered to get dressed but threw a parka over pajamas and headed outdoors. Sometimes the bears come very close to the ship, perhaps smelling the cooking of the next meal or perhaps from curiosity. It is always a thrill when a bear approaches and you can photograph it so close by. It is amazing to hear its grunts and observe the foggy breath emanating from its nostrils. A bear's large feet, great for propelling it as it swims, allow for great stability and stealth as it patrols the ice. Viewing a polar bear in the wild is an exhilarating experience for all.

The polar bear may eat only once every eight days, so after dining on a seal, it can be very patient when hunting for its next. Although seals are the most abundant and the bears' favorite prey, they also eat beluga whales and walrus. The bears are often seen on their bellies with front paws extended while watching a breathing or exit hole for the seal. When a seal pops its head up through the ice to breathe, the bear grabs it by the head and tosses it backwards to kill the unsuspecting animal. The polar bear will either devour the seal at the site or drag the carcass elsewhere. It is not unusual to see blood trails along the ice floes. We have seen many sights of predation throughout the world, but as difficult as these kills are to watch, we understand the cycle of life.

When disembarking on Zodiacs for hiking and viewing birds, scenery, or potentially bears in the Arctic where danger may be an issue, the crew leaves the ship first with loaded rifles. They separate and form a circle of protection should a bear appear. In that case the crew would shoot their weapons in the air to hopefully dissuade the bears from approaching the ship's passengers. It is almost counterproductive to spot a bear when we're on land. Once a bear is sighted, we all must immediately return to the ship. On land, you cannot get close to these huge, dangerous creatures. Our best photos are taken from the expedition ship with long lenses.

Walruses are much easier to photograph but are also challenging to find. As they are not aggressive if the tourist is respectful of their territory and do not try to come close enough to create discomfort for the animal, you can get within 50 or 100 yards of these large sea beasts. These mammals are found in the area of the North Pole and the Arctic Ocean, and are easily identified by their large tusks, flippers, and size. The walrus may weigh 4,000 pounds! Their unique tusks are used to dig prey from the sea bottom and to assist them when climbing from the water back onto the ice. The walrus dines on shrimp and other mollusks such as crab and clams. We see the walrus on ice floes, both alone and in herds, floating by with the wind and current, oblivious to our presence. When a group is spotted on a beach, we disembark far from the animals and hike back to view them. We try to stay very quiet and low and to find an ice ridge behind which we can shoot our pictures. Some walruses remain stationary while others slide into and out of the sea.

WOLVES

WE ALWAYS ENJOY PHOTOGRAPHING WOLVES, BOTH IN THE WILD and in rescue centers across the country. Wolves, which in the past could be found throughout the United States, are most apt to be seen in the northern states bordering Canada, including Alaska. Yellowstone National Park is a great area in which to view these interesting creatures. We have also visited the International Wolf Center in Ely, Minnesota, and Lakota Wolf Preserve in Columbia, New Jersey.

The gray wolf, also known as the timber wolf, lives in remote areas and is the largest in the wolf family. Its fur is usually mottled gray and brown (although colors may range from white to black) and it is long, dense, and bushy. Males can weigh 100 pounds. As with most wolves, they live in a social group or pack of up to a dozen animals. They are territorial and protect their area with scent marking and howling.

The arctic wolf, usually white, is a medium-sized animal that is a subspecies of the gray wolf. They are found in the higher latitudes of North America (Alaska, Canada) and Greenland. As they are not fearful of humans, they some-

times approach those around research stations in the wild. These wolves prey on lemmings, birds, arctic foxes, caribou, and muskoxen. Their ears are smaller than other wolves for heat retention, their coats are well adapted for bitter cold, and they thrive despite the winter months in darkness. The size of their pack is dependent upon the availability of food.

The British Columbia wolf is another subspecies of the gray wolf that lives in an area from the temperate Vancouver, British Columbia, to southeast Alaska. Their coat is very dark, ranging from a rusty dark red to black. Their prey includes moose, caribou, sheep, deer, beavers, and bison. They prefer open tundra and forests, and their packs can have between two and 30 members. These wolves are endangered, with conservation and reintroduction programs offering them a chance at long-term survival.

One of our most memorable experiences while visiting the Lakota Wolf Preserve occurred when our guide encouraged one of the arctic wolves to howl. Within a few seconds, all the wolves in the preserve joined in howling. As we had a small digital recorder with us, we were able to memorialize

the extraordinary vocalizations of these magnificent animals. We played the recording for our own dogs who immediately became alerted to the new sounds. They spent several minutes staring at the recorder apparently trying to understand what they were hearing.

EPILOGUE

COMBINING OUR LOVE OF ANIMALS AND THE PRIVILEGE WE HAVE TO travel and view them in the wild has been one of the most rewarding experiences of our lives. Each time we travel, we gain new knowledge of the countries and residents we visit. It has always been a treat to share our experiences, both in terms of photographs and the stories of our most memorable observations. During our summer art shows, we are encouraged by those who visit our booth, who ask questions about our photos and enjoy the stories behind the images. Our website contains hundreds of our images, and although the stories related to those images are not shared there, we encourage those who wish to know more about any picture to contact us, either by email or phone. We firmly believe that the story makes the image more meaningful!

We plan to continue to travel for as long as we are able and to share our photographs and adventures. There are still many places, sights, and animals we would like to visit and observe. We welcome any suggestions in planning our future travels. We post our summer fair schedule on our website and Facebook page as we formulate our plans. We would encourage those who are able to visit us at one of our weekly shows, and although we do not expect our visitors to "carry our luggage," we hope that our conversations will encourage everyone who can to seize the opportunity to explore the world and the world of animals whenever possible.

We try to share our respect and appreciation for the animals living across our planet in such a way that we effectively communicate the promotion of conservation of wildlife. We all have a responsibility to participate in ways that ensure that all species of animals and their habitats will remain for future generations.

Please visit our website at compassroseimages.com, where our photos may be viewed and purchased as greeting cards, tiles (ceramic coasters and trivets), matted prints, gallery wrap canvas, and on high-definition metal. We ship throughout the US, Canada, UK, Australia, and New Zealand at this time. Please contact us for shipping rates to other countries or territories.

We welcome the opportunity to share our photographs and stories with groups as well. Should your group be interested in a presentation, please contact us for further information and scheduling.

Thank you for giving us the opportunity to share our passion for wildlife with you. Please visit our website, where new photos are added frequently as our travels continue.

SHELLEY LANCE-FULK & JACKLYN AMTOWER

Compass Rose Images

compassroseimages.com